THE BURNING OF THE BOOKS
AND OTHER POEMS

George Szirtes was born in Budapest in 1948, and came to England with his family after the 1956 Hungarian Uprising. He was educated in England, training as a painter, and has always written in English. In recent years he has worked as a translator of Hungarian literature. He retired from teaching at the University of East Anglia in 2003, and lives in Wymondham, Norfolk.

His first collection, *The Slant Door*, was awarded the Geoffrey Faber Prize, and since then he has won the T.S. Eliot Prize and a Cholmondeley Award and been shortlisted for Whitbread and Forward Poetry Prizes. He was elected a Fellow of the Royal Society of Literature in 1982.

After his first return to Hungary in 1984 he translated poetry, fiction and plays from the Hungarian and for his work in this field he has won the European Poetry Translation Prize, the Dery Prize and been shortlisted for the Weidenfeld and Aristeion Prizes as well as receiving the Golden Star medal of the Hungarian republic. His translation of László Krasznahorkai's Satantango won the Best Translated Book Award in 2013, and was a Man Booker International winner in 2015, as translator of László Krasznahorkai.

With George Gömöri he co-edited Bloodaxe's *The Colonnade of Teeth: Modern Hungarian Poetry* (1996), and his Bloodaxe edition of Ágnes Nemes Nagy's poetry, *The Night of Akhenaton: Selected Poems* (2004), was a Poetry Book Society Recommended Translation. His study of the artist Ana Maria Pacheco, *Exercise of Power*, was published by Ashgate in 2001. He co-edited *An Island of Sound: Hungarian Poetry and Fiction before and beyond the Iron Curtain* (Harvill, 2004) and *In Their Own Words: Contemporary Poets on their Poetry* (Salt, 2012).

His Bloodaxe poetry titles include: *The Budapest File* (2000); *An English Apocalypse* (2001); *Reel* (2004), winner of the T.S. Eliot Prize; *New & Collected Poems* (2008); *The Burning of the Books and other poems* (2009); *Bad Machine* (2013); and *Mapping the Delta* (2016). *The Burning of the Books* and *Bad Machine* were both shortlisted for the T.S. Eliot Prize. *Bad Machine* and *Mapping the Delta* are both Poetry Book Society Choices. Bloodaxe has also published his Newcastle/Bloodaxe Poetry Lectures, *Fortinbras at the Fishhouses: Responsibility, the Iron Curtain and the sense of history as knowledge* (2010), and John Sears' critical study, *Reading George Szirtes* (2008). His memoir of his mother, *The Photographer at Sixteen*, was published by MacLehose Press in 2019.

GEORGE SZIRTES

THE BURNING OF THE BOOKS

AND OTHER POEMS

BLOODAXE BOOKS

ISBN: 978 1 85224 842 0

First published 2009 by
Bloodaxe Books Ltd,
Eastburn,
South Park,
Hexham,
Northumberland NE46 1BS.

www.bloodaxebooks.com
For further information about Bloodaxe titles
please visit our website and join our mailing list
or write to the above address for a catalogue.

Supported by
ARTS COUNCIL
ENGLAND

Cover design: Neil Astley & Pamela Robertson-Pearce.

This is a digital reprint of the 2009 Bloodaxe edition.

For RONALD KING, 'the Pozzo of the printed page', begetter, collaborator, publisher and artist of *The Burning of the Books*,

And for PETER SCUPHAM, who wrote:

The problem is, how to disfigure moonlight
And keep the accidentals of the moon,
The onceness and the hand-in-hand of it

('The Mechanicals')

...all the accidentals.

ACKNOWLEDGEMENTS

'Chet Baker' was published in *The Irish Times*; 'Lead White', *The Penig Film* and 'Apropos Palladio' appeared in *Manhattan Review*; *The Burning of the Books* was first published by Circle Press. *In the Face of History: In Time of War* was commissioned by the Barbican Gallery, London, seven of the poems from it appearing in *Poetry*; *Northern Air: A Hungarian Nova Zembla* was commissioned by BBC Radio 4 and was first published in *The Hungarian Quarterly*; *Songs of the Wrestler József Szabó* first appeared in *The Rialto* who also published 'White Noise'; all the prose poems first appeared in *Almost Island* (India); *A Howard Hodgkin Suite* first appeared in *The London Magazine*; some of the canzones appeared first in *Guernica* and in *The Salzburg Review*; *The Birds* sequence was published in *The International Literary Review*; *Pools* and *The Man Who Wove Grass* were published in *.Cent*; 'Pontormo' first appeared in *Poetry Review*, 'The Translators' in *The Rialto*; a version of 'Woolworths' on the *Peony Moon* website; 'Bathing and Singing', 'However' and 'Primavera' in *10x3* (USA).

CONTENTS

Chet Baker

Somewhere at the far end of the hall
In a year you can't remember,
So far away it might have been yesterday,
A voice begins to fall.

Nothing but pathos across a certain distance
That vanishes as soon as heard,
But keeps falling, a wan thin voice
Incapable, it seems, of resistance...

It is only gravity after all, the sound
Of a horn whose very echo fades
In falling. But, God, to be falling
Like that all the way to the ground

And be littered with broken phrases
Even as air clears and smoke rises.

Lead White

1

Sometimes the world just wants to twist
through your fingers and will not be held:
the way your cat writhes in your arms,
the washing that blows away in a huge gust
from nowhere, all the billowing forms
of water that suddenly rise and thrust
themselves in your face, the clouds that blank
out the healing sun. The table set for the meal
topples over, the chair-back snaps, and the dank
ceiling drops lath and plaster into your heart...
      Sometimes you feel the presence of God, his hand
gently pushing down on you, and you start
a thought that is partly an ache, as if you could heal
the world with all the goodness you sense
in the cat or the washing, in whatever escapes you,
for everything in the world is good: it is his presence
in the leaping writhing thing, it is the way he shapes you
to his purpose; for he hates injustice and will marry,
if need be, the harlot and restore her to virginity;
for his love can support the humble and despised,
descending with miners into the pit of hell
or toiling in fields with peasants while the bell
booms in the distance in the deep well of his charity,
in the village tower, in forsakenness and penury.
And the yellow figure advancing towards you is Christ,
and the world twists and leaps like the cat that won't
be held in your hands and the washing that billows
against cloud and brilliant sky, past the furrows
of the field, past the stream with its constant
restlessness, everything moving beyond you
at an impossible rate, twisting, rattling through.

2

Yes, there are starry nights and cafés that lurch
out of some melancholy stupor in the four A.M.
consciousness. There is something seismic in the church
that billows and buckles, its stones a grey flame
blown this way and that. Restlessness marks

the darkness where we sit, the table at which we eat.
I watch the eaters, the toilers, the man who works
in the village delivering post, the crooked street
that wriggles ahead of us. I would prefer to seize
the precise moment when grass blows
all one way as if it had an intention,
the moment before wind-tugged petals close
for the night. I am searching for the proper tension
between God and his world, in the purr of the pigeon,
in the floating world of *ukiyo-e*, in the glum
alleys of Doré's London, in the voice of Spurgeon
resounding and challenging both crowded slum
and fancy hotel. I am Vincent. Let me introduce
myself. I am the name you will learn to pronounce.
I have a mission. I will build my own cross
and hang from it. It is my due, my penance.

3

Once upon a time, in the acidic piss-yellow gloom
of a half-empty billiard room
I had a vision of a clock full of poison, a nagging green
presence emerging from behind a screen.
I counted the tables. There were few of them remaining.
Time was on its way out, its hands straining
to break free, to strangle the hour. The lamps winnowed
flakes of thick light. Their energy flowed
through and shook me. I had the shakes. I had bad dreams.
I thought I could hear the screams
of empty bottles, the idiotic grunting of fuel
in the stove. I heard the cruel
laughter of the glasses tinkling behind the desolate bar
with its blob of flowers, each pink smear
a parody of flesh. A man stood by the billiard table,
staring at me. I was mad, unstable,
uncertain of my footing. The cue is pointing at me.
I stare back. I put down what I see.

4

I put down what I see: a boat, a windmill, several
windmills. I am after all a Dutchman. I see wind
as a block of lead-white as it falls forward
into my head. I scumble it around, making clouds

13

froth up. I sink the street in it. Now everything is stiff
with a plastered-down melancholy. The sails rise
and fall, churning away at the world. Material
things: these dense, butt-heavy folds of happening.

5

The folds of the world are heavy. One strains
to support them. The cat, the washing, the walls
of the church, the will of God, panes
of glass that pretend to be eyes, all heavy.
I wrestle with this heaviness. I raise
the sails of the windmill. Time stalls,
refuses to budge. Sometimes it sticks for days
and I must lie here in a kind of reverie
watching the chair assemble itself into a cry,
a golden cry that comes straight out of the sun.
Meanwhile the poor potter about or stand
stock-still by cottage doors. They die
away from me. They can't understand
my piety. They fade, shuffle away, entering
the thick slab of sky, the white cake
of the clouds, light's curious wobbling
across river and field. They leave me to ache
with their absence, their intensity
of being, their sheer density.

6

Once I loved the poetry of words
but now it is the poetry of the intractable
that moves me: the hovering of birds
above a field, the windmill's terrible
sails droning in the gale, the taste of white lead,
the narrowness of a room with its single bed,
the quarrel with a close friend,
the fury of the provincial alley
late at night, the mind's dead end.

7

And then it all glows with the fury of the sun:
the alley bursts like a vein
in an explosion of light, as if light were rain
fractured into drops that run

14

down the inside of the eye and the field springs
to attention, the sunflower glares,
the trees twist and grow improbable wings.
In the provincial town squares
fizz like hotplates. Mind grows chambers like
the heart and, all clumsiness
forgotten, learns to lilt, dance and strike
light into the world, to bless
the place where God sits: the emptiness.

THE BURNING OF THE BOOKS

1 *Prologue*

When he had gathered all the books

When he had indexed, catalogued, cross-referred and annotated them
When the little princelings and mighty emperors of China
Were dancing on the pinpoint of his own estimable head
And the bile of the world was swimming in the gutters
And the fists of the janitor were beating street girls black and blue
And the oleaginous salesman had lubricated the hinges of the *cassone*
For the delectation of the housekeeper
A tiny gale started blowing
Down the alleyways and through the portals
Through the flightless windows
Through the wainscoted corridors of the *rathaus*
And the Groszbeggars stirred and shook a leg
And the Dixwounded rattled their small change of limbs
And acrobats stood on their heads like stars
And there were murders
Murders and conspiracies
For the intellect to catalogue and classify
For the mind to annotate and the fingers to cross-refer
For a superior consciousness to make sense of
In the hallways and beer cellars
In the prisons and surgeries
In lavatories and libraries

Where the books were gathered.

Where books are gathered there gathers also the dust
That sieves through the pores of the skin and the head,
The absolute dust of the language that falls apart
In your hands, that settles in your palm
Like a promise. Ideas are dust. Words dust,
A universe of dust between planet and planet,
Precious dust certainly, gold dust, a dusting
Of light filtered through eyelashes batting over
The damp-smelling page, the foxing, the marginals,
The improvised shopping list of the dead,
The dead themselves, the dust of the prisons,
The workhouses of dust, the dust bowl, the dustbin
Of history, the dust of the poor who have wasted away
Into particles, molecules, atoms, the dust of the birds
In their nests, the dust of the hotel where the dwarf
And the scholar fossick among motes
Among invisible books, the books of the imagination,
The trapped dust of the folded page, the folded umbrella,
The folds of the skin that are clogged with dust,
The dust of the ovens to come, the dust of the scouring pad,
The citizens of dust in the dusty streets,
The dust of the city you shake off your sandals,
The dust mites, the silverfish of the imagination,
The dust of the station where a speech is in progress,
The dust of the mountain pass with its butchered soldiers.

Librarian of the universal library, have you explored
The shelves in the stockroom where the snipers are sitting,
The repository of landmines in the parking bay,
The suspicious white powder at the check-out desk,
The mysterious rays bombarding you by the photocopier,
The psychological disorder of the filing system
That governs the paranoid republic of print
In the wastes of the world?

Once she had passed over the kid gloves
And the book appeared with its antiquary bloom,
Its insect words pinned into place with light,
It was clear there was expense involved.
Expense and respect, and a question of property.
I don't deal with property. I am a scholar.
I don't do housekeeping. I don't do money.
I do the rounds of the bookshops, interrogating
Dealers with rare editions in long-lost languages.
I have circumnavigated the alleys of Berlin
More often than I can remember, but I recall
Perfectly the place of each book on each shelf
And have marked its neighbours and condition.
Money is air. I breathe it in and out.
I blow my nose clear of it. I piss it in the morning
And last thing at night. Money is the slight breeze
Playing round my temples as I enter the shop,
The slight draught at my back as I leave it.
It is a whisper of fallen leaves in the gutter,
The rustle half-dry and half-damp of a system in decay.
Pass me the kid gloves. I am handling a book.
The words of the dead are settling over me.
I drift among them, weightless, like a balloon
Floating on helium, looking down on gutters
Overflowing with leaves and paper money.
I don't see the difference.

You'd take me for one of the pawns of history
But I'm a strategist and will bet you a thousand
The pawns hold their own in the struggle that's coming.
Lie down with me here in the brothel, under the bed
Where the wife works, and concentrate on this board,
Not on the one above you where the simple grinding
Of bodies gets nobody anywhere, except in a mess
That has to be laundered, with occasional diseases
And temporary relief. I may be a dwarf of mere pawn size,
My back may be hunched but my mind is perfectly clear.
I have studied the openings, gambits and end-games
And have them located in places you can't see
In the tidy formal gardens of the mind, in dwarf hedges,
Down microscopic walks, in all but invisible orangeries,
In mazes and charming terminal follies.
I have sat with the Shah, playing automatons,
Considered the nightingale and the edge of the scimitar,
I have dashed into alleys when the knights came looking
On their hooked courses when the castles ganged up on me.
I can take out dividers and measure the distance
From front line to end row, to point of transformation:
From dwarf with bone back-pack to queen in manoeuvres
Beyond the average prole (how few of them make it!).
Others may rattle on about ideology,
Others write pamphlets or organise meetings,
Others may fight on the barricades, raise banners, assassinate,
And you, my friend, insist on your invisible books
Your empty orangeries. My books are Morphy and Alekhine.
We walk through the garden together, down geometric paths.
Go on. Make your first move. Push your pawn forward
And let's leave them rocking above us.

No sooner can a child walk and make out his letters
Than he is surrendered to the hard pavement
Of any ill-built street where others are skipping
In squares among grids that are numbered
Or leaping through ropes, screaming incoherencies,
Under systems of stars that are inexplicable,
Past policemen with batons and revolvers in their holsters,
In the stern light of midday between short hard-edged shadows
That cut them in two so that half is invisible
Or else dazzled, and no one can make out the letters
Of street signs, of names on shop windows, of notices in the park
Or even begin to discriminate between delicate shades
Of small print in the sheet of newspaper blown along the gutter.
No sooner can a child walk than he has to start running
And bones that are brittle get broken so that he must read
The harsh rules of the body, its blood, flesh and skin,
The codes inscribed in the nerve-cells he has inherited
From nameless uncles, from fly-by-night affairs
That establish the book of his being, the fool's idiolect
He must speak all his life. Ideas are eternal
And even the match I hold to this page is impotent
Because this very moment someone is remembering
The syntax and rhythm of phrases that have detached themselves
From flammable editions, and the grammar keeps reforming
Hurtling down the street where the child plays
And stumbles, blowing in his face like a paper bag
Adhering to his features, so when he peels it away
The face remains there, its features encrypted
Then flies past him into libraries, into volumes of speech
No one can hear or pronounce.

It was the two black, calm, sad eyes I was watching
As they rose above the majestic nose, looking over it
As a guard might look down from his tower
With a certain sadness at the landscape retreating before him
Into the infinite distance, where somewhere, his family
Were busily queueing in shops or exchanging news.
It was the two black, calm, sad eyes that got me
As they were bound to. I thought of my father
And of the long tunnel descending into the pit
Of himself and our history, whose entrance lay
In the pupils and the confusing cavity
Of his nostrils that also must lead somewhere
As do all orifices including those in the earth
Where it's cold and *unheimlich* and where are laid
Those with similar eyes, noses and mouths.
        And then I noticed the hump that was almost all
Of his body, the curved hill that looped from the sacrum
And over the shoulders, descending into the neck
With violent force as if to push the same sacrum
Back down into earth, but then his mouth twittered,
Something moved between lips, I heard the dwarf language
Swell into cadences larger than he was. Soon he was singing,
A deep bass voice, like the voice of my father,
The voice breaking, not perfectly focused or tuned.
It is that singing I listen to most of the time
When I see him, those black, calm, sad eyes of his
And that majestic nose growing ever more majestic
As if to balance the hump on the other side.

And so she adjusted the hang of the starched blue skirt
Expanding its hard umbrella into the rain
Of shadows that spread right over the carpet.
Money no object. Everything in its right place.
Just add a few noughts. Still on the right side of fifty.
These were her songs sung to the worn accordion
Pumping away in her lungs and the broken violin
Of her bodice, each a respectable tune, fit for a person
Accustomed to order. And order expanded
From its core in her person, the opening wings
Of the umbrella, the terrifying skirt, the raw starch.
     And under the skirt the raw muscle snapped into place
Supporting the hips and the waist and everything above it
So the structure was firm and impervious to weather,
The gales that blew in her mind, the drizzle of commentary
On the shortcomings of employers and husbands,
On the vulgarity of women younger than herself,
On the patterns made by the rain at her feet
Till the starched blue skirt was already half metal,
Not just the ribs but the fabric, and started to clang
Like a bell each time she touched it, each time
The rain beat on it, so everything was ringing:
Just add a few noughts. Still on the right side of fifty,
And the bells of the city were ecstasy, the clangour
Pealing out hours, days, weeks, months until time itself
Was exhausted but still on the right side of fifty,
And the rain finally stopped, the clouds swam off
Into the distance and the terrible sunlight
Of certainty settled across her and across the city
The shadows much sharper, the brightness alarming.

Our life is furniture, though the table doesn't exist
Off which master and servant may eat and imagine
Themselves equals. Nor can the bed where we sleep
Support the idea of our persons, our accoutrements,
Our fine silk pyjamas and ratty underwear,
Without being assured of our proper positions.
The divan is hard, she complained. I say nothing.
I have my memories, and memory is the chair
I have sat in, the carpet I sweep, the sideboard I stock,
The wardrobe I polish with soft cloth, rough hands and this wax.
     I have walked down dark art nouveau corridors, have run my hands
Over regency card-tables: I have entered through doors
That are panelled, rooms that are coffered. I have
The furniture of my heart arranged into pleasing patterns,
But this furniture is what is appropriate to a person
Of my class and upbringing. I have stood at the windows
Of expensive establishments, measured up suites
And toyed with the thought of a chaise longue curled
Like a petal. The furniture of my dreams is equally organic
And I at the centre, the queen of the garden,
A species of moth fluttering between flowerbeds
And that bright piece of glass now catching the sunlight.
Each day in silence we eat our lunch, we break our bread,
We furnish our thoughts with resentments and hopes.
The delicate flower of my chair swallows me:
I am seated and swallowed by that which I sit in,
This city, this silence, these books, my age and my station.

To eat books is to have a stomach full of corners,
Because the word is angular and has sharp edges
That cut you: consonants, sibilants, gutturals,
No sound is free from danger, everything harms you.
Say you lie on the pavement, pounding your fists
Against concrete, someone will come along and loose
Razor-sharp words at your ear. Your ears begin bleeding
And soon your mind and your heart are bloody,
For we are sensitive creatures we lovers of language,
Said the scholar. Yes, we spout nonsense and turn
Talk into knives, but there is a higher order of knowledge.
We are stupid, we splutter, we indulge infatuations,
Loving those who despise us, the dwarf considered,
And money is money. There is no truth in the world
And this nose and these eyes are agents of strategy
As much as the hump I carry on my back, for between
Books and money, between abstraction and flesh
There are oceans of blood, blood on the chess-board
Where the pieces are restless, blood on the parcel
You carry to assignments, blood on the contracts
You present to your workforce and never a book
Lodged in their stomachs, for their stomachs being empty,
What they require is cash and food and a piece
Of flesh to be squeezing or eating. It is ourselves
Not the books we eat, our bodies are nourishment
Beyond words or symbols or letters or paper.
A thin man survives on a colophon. I am a thin man,
The scholar replied: colophons, indexes, chapter headings.
Life is annotation. Hunger and annotation. It is knowledge
We hunger for, letters we drink, desire in our bloodstream
For the fat, visceral, blood-bound flesh of our books.

The crowd falls upon whomsoever it pleases to fall on
And can sniff out a criminal as if by instinct,
So the instinct radiates, spreads like rays of the sun
That enter the skin and penetrate to the bones
Which are guilty, guilty by virtue of difference,
Smelling of roses or stagnant water, thick with hot goods,
And then they are done for, no matter how petty
The acts once committed, the pinchpenny perjury,
The lost book, the slightest waste of expensive breath
Recorded somewhere in the files of the bones,
In the databank of marrow down at the station
Where stragglers are questioned and punished,
And so the crowd moves on, culprit by culprit, until the guilty
Are cornered and given a good kicking. The streets
Even now are records of blood and boot marks,
The shopfronts and entrances breathe with the ghosts
Of those who once stood there, carrying something
As heavy as bones secreted within their culpable bodies
While the crowd passes unconscious of being a crowd,
A mere tick from the welter in the alley
That even now is filing towards the square
Where squats the Theresianum with its dealers
Proceeding lawfully without a thought of murder
Or theft, but the books will tell of it, point to the murderers
And protest aloud against thieves, their mouths wide
And yelling out, crying *Stop thief! Stop thief!* and *Constable,
Murder!* In Vienna, in Rome, there is murder and theft
And the smell of roses and the troubling stench
Of stagnant water. Fishwife and dwarf, blind man and scholar,
Listen, they're after you, they've broken into a run,
The wind takes them by the hand, the sun radiates their bones.

The point about the madhouse is that it's virile.
The point about the madhouse is that it sticks by its beliefs.
The point about the madhouse is that sanity is bourgeois.
The point about the madhouse is that no one is acting.
The point about the madhouse is that no one gets in by simply being nice.
The point about the madhouse is that it liberates the spirit.
The point about the madhouse is that you can think just what you like there.
The point about the madhouse is that anyone can enter.
There's nothing special about the madhouse, people come and go all the time.
There's nothing threatening about the madhouse, we are all of us dying.
There's nothing terminal about the madhouse: you go along for the ride.
There's nothing sad about the madhouse: weeping and gnashing of teeth,
        that's nothing.
There's nothing mad about the madhouse, it is sanity by default.
We are sane by default, we are mad by design, but the mad are more admirable.
Admirable is the ape, the bulbul, the mitochondrion, the swelling of the larynx,
Admirable the orchid, the garlic, the fire inside the shut book,
Admirable the cry of the tortured, the lost voice of the nightingale, the laughter
In everything ostensibly sane but tending towards madness
Such as sunlight, the slow rain, each pendulous drop, the wide road,
The brimming eye, shadows, picnics, public conveyances, thunder.
Nature is a madness with a method and all the madder for that.
Culture is a madness everyone inherits.
Science is a madness in love with numbers, the perfect *amour fou.*
Health is a madness that shifts from minute to minute, *gesundheit!*
Money is madness that fills your pockets and leaves a silver slugtrail in the garden.
The point about the madhouse is not to describe it.
The point about the madhouse is not to change it.
The point about the madhouse is to live there,
To accustom yourself to its immaculate manners,
To dwell in the house of the Lord for ever
With the prophet, the poet, the dwarf, the scholar, the fire.

Consider the hard blue skirt. Consider the ancients.
Consider the sheer raw animality you hardly knew
Till you dreamt it in the flesh. And so you enter the flesh
And know it corrupt. You are entering nothing.
It is deceit and luxury and when you lay hands on them
They die like the pressure at the back of your head.
Consider the flesh. Are you not better off without it?
Are you not pure word, pure accumulation of silence
In the explosion of your books, whereas they –
The greedy, the grasping self-sacrificers, the hoarders
Of hurt, wearers of paint, smoothers out of skin, wooers
Of the mirrored lust that shows you within them, where
There is nothing – they, the pure vessels of tears as murky
As washing, they are slatterns, voluptuaries, murderers
Of the truth with their blue mountainous, bell-like skirts,
Who read but six pages of *The Trousers of Herr von Bredow*
Only to assume control of a world of trousers.
I once knew a man all fists, his knuckles were hungry
And he did not hesitate to lay about with them,
A man with a wife and a daughter, both of them dead,
The man who had been a policeman known as Ginger the Cat,
Around him a desert of beggars and trousers,
My keeper, my likeness, my flipside, my fury, my hoarse
Obliging servant, red in the face. I think of the skirt
Ringing to his touch, I think of the ancients,
Of Delilah, Clytemnestra, Penelope, Cleopatra,
The short sharp shock of grief, a miasma of perfume.
I have no body but fire and my fire purges them,
They are ashes and pages, fluttering tongues of light.

The sadness of brown paper is an imaginary sadness
But no less real for that, for there it is spread over the floor
Like flakes of linoleum, linoleum of all things being assuredly the saddest,
Especially brown linoleum, its brownness signifying an autumn of the spirit,
Those autumnal books, the foxed blotches of your words in the distance
Curling and damp and shiny as the leaf settling into the mud
Of the field, words and leaves, words and mud, autumn
In the library of the cheap intermediate, transitional, improvised room
In the missing heart of the world, its shelves cleared of everything
But imagination. But the imagination of man is wicked, says the word
Of the god in the lobby, whose footsteps are even now to be heard
Ascending the stairs. He is waiting at the door, his finger on the buzzer,
As he brings you the book of the skin translucent as moonlight
Through blinds. It is midnight. It is autumn. Brown paper is spread
Across the sofa and over the carpet, it is sad; and the mind
Must heave out its load of precious knowledge and do its own binding
Carefully wrapping the bulk of the invisible in the brown paper
Of the autumnal, damply glistening in the sad light
Of the hotel where the moon hovers a moment then enters a package,
Settling between pages that cannot be seen or read or sold
But must hold the virtual spaces of the world together,
Mend it with punctuation, indent its impossible paragraphs
And present it as an achievement, properly wrapped, tied round with string
As the proceeds of autumn, its sweepings, its accumulations tidied
Into a pile at the full heart of the book where it rises to a point,
Dries, goes stiff, fragile and papery and before you know it
Someone has put a match to it to send tiny black birds of ash
Drifting across the terrain of the mind in the mood of the moment,
Fire and winter, the withered tree burning with fire at its centre.

To dream of books is to dream of men and to dream of men
Is to dream of God, of sages burning in God's holy fire,
Of Pentecostal flames above the mouths of apostles,
Of a live coal placed on the lips of the prophet, of a wholesale
Burning of books, such as here, here on this very street
Where they are piled high. We shall make them eat their words,
Cry the ringleaders, they shall speak with tongues of fire,
They shall write on the page of the tongue, and we shall set wild cats
On them, tigers, leopards, jaguars, minxes and they shall tear their books,
Each book's breath rising from its chest in a hot draught,
Its ideas blackening and curling into a forgotten language
Of ash and smoke that is even now rising over the city,
And this is the book of the dream that is also the book
Of the book, each voice curling and blackening, unique
And forgotten, and the jaguars stalk the night streets
The onion-paper of their eyes flickering and thin,
The small print of their teeth gathering in the margin,
The index of their jaws containing everything possible to be written,
The codicil of their tails disappearing on the unlit pavement.
This was the book of my dream, the scholar exclaimed
On waking, these books were my people, these cracked spines
Their sacrum and vertebrae, these jaguars the priests
Of the ignorant, and the fire, the fire is ambiguous
But may be interpreted by a careful close reading,
By a proper classification of the texts referred to,
By a single marginal comment sharp as a tooth,
By a course of intensive study in the appropriate libraries,
Those burning places of the intellect, those driers out
Of the eyes where barbarians gather with their torches
And rank upon rank of shelves, tongues and footnotes
Are burning as always, as is their nature, in the streets
Of the city that opens like a book and must itself always be burning.

Canzone: Architecture
(for Marilyn Hacker)

Somewhere there is a perfect architecture
where light, form, shadow, space all move
to form a language beyond architecture,
where to dream of the wrong architecture
is to dream of dying. But waking bans
the dream and reinvents the architecture
of the empty day that is all architecture
and no dream. Is there somewhere a culprit
we might blame for this, and is the culprit
ourselves? We make our own architecture
and live in it as in a house of ill fame
it being all we desire of fame.

Our fame is inward: it is a private fame
for which we must create an architecture
of outwardness if only because fame
cannot remain private if it is to be fame.
We know our names and must pronounce the bans
from the pulpit of our anonymous fame.
Who can object to this? It is our own fame
we give names to, couple with and move
house with. It is ourselves we move
and no one else. We proclaim our fame
to the walls that recognise a culprit
when they hear one: name itself is culprit.

And what, after all, is it to be a culprit?
It is to have a certain portion of fame
and take it for self, blaming the culprit
for desire to survive merely as a culprit.
It is the self building an architecture
in which it may be possible to be a culprit.
But who could bear always to be a culprit,
a culprit, what is more, at one remove
beyond the self, unable to move
a culprit in a pulpit perhaps but still a culprit,
subject therefore to all the usual bans,
both hating and welcoming such bans?

There's a certain kind of building the city bans,
the builder of which it treats as a culprit,
applying not only these but other bans,
because cities depend on applying bans
in case the rampant self obscures the fame
due only to cities. Order dictates bans:
bans dictate anonymity. No one bans
no one. None may construct the architecture
that is merely a building calling itself architecture.
The self may bar itself against some bans
but no self can afford to stay still. It must move.
There's always another building, one more move.

Self is an architecture that must move
in order to accommodate. No self bans
movement because it knows that to move
is to survive. Heart must beat, blood move
around the building. To live is to be a culprit.
And then another enters with a neat move
slick as a poem that is obliged to move
the heart, which is all a self can know of fame,
bestowing fame through accommodation. *Fame
at last* is words like these, constantly on the move
turning the building into architecture
or simply calling the building architecture.

I touch the miraculous architecture
of your face feeling its own solitary fame
knowing myself both self and culprit.
Something inside the word rebels, bans
conversation. It's language on the move.

THE PENIG FILM

1 *Clio at the film festival*

This is a small thing, wound down to a few
inches, running across your life on the screen
you stare at when you have nothing else to do.

It's a little grey patch no more than that, the scene
of one of a million crimes that are over
in a blink of Clio's eyes, Clio who does not mean

to get personal with you, or to blow her cover
as an allegorical personage by engaging
in dialectics or gossip. You are not her lover

after all, merely a figure she meets while staging
one of her periodic out-takes in an ordinary place
on cheap location. She does not go about raging

or tearing her mythical hair. Her peculiar grace
is inimitable in its indifference. She does not
believe in getting involved. As for your face

that's your own business: profile, mug shot
the whole Boltansky effect, it's not her bag,
she'll not light a candle for you, or reserve a spot

among her unnamed extras. You can't blag
your way onto her payroll by telling it as it is.
It's what appears in the movie that matters. You drag

your small space with you through the various cities
of the imagination that she has filmed to scale
complete with a starry cast of iconic celebrities.

Here we are, says Clio. This sad square of pale
grey is yours, set the figures in motion. Write
your own script as the lights begin to fail.

Go on working in the dark, in the long night
of the empty cinema, I'll leave you to it now.
I must catch my beauty sleep. I have an early flight.

So the figures start moving any old how,
faintly shivering, in a precarious state
of preservation. Billow little flames, allow

us to breathe our lives into yours, create
our insignificant masterpiece for us,
be actors and ushers, offer us templates

we may apply to our more decorous
viewing. Speak the speeches trippingly
without tripping, sing to us in chorus,

whisper individual secrets, now singly,
now in pairs, in rows, in tiers. Become
familiars, behave yourselves, be fittingly

that which propriety requires, the tidy sum
of tidy greynesses in an official film, shot
by army officers on an afternoon, glum

as the century's mood, emerging from your cot
of earth, mud, lime and bone, to rise, or be carried
to a hospital from the place Clio forgot

to visit, deloused, de-starved, and de-buried,
wrapped in your flimsy nightwear of memory
drifting into consciousness, into the unhurried

pace of a life that is other, into this shimmery
surface where light is diffused across a rectangle
that jolts and jolts as it passes through the century.

There are ghosts that know no walls, flames that mingle
with smoke, smoke that drifts into cloud, cloud that thins
into a sky of monolithic blue whose single

idea is a clean start and then nothing. It begins
and ends like this. The show is over. The light
of day and the absence of light, a thousand pins

of lesser light. The stars are out tonight.
You hear them purring like an old projector
stuttering images, a spattered black and white.

You name them by pinpointing the sector
they once occupied. You entice them to speak
as images can, without a lie detector,

trembling at skin and bone, pressing the weak
against the wall, all nakedness and shame.
You seek that which is always hard to seek.

3 *Birth*

Let's begin with dust, one tiny frame,
a speck floating anywhere, let us say, here,
in a room like this, a place you can claim

as your own, whose blind-spot of fear
avoids your focus. Mother cries. Shoves
and breaks, and there you are, in the clear,

at the very beginning, where hand moves
to skull and mouth to breast and milk flows
between lips. Stars settle in wild droves

over the roof. They're amazing. Life goes
to your head. You're drunk on it. The child
is right beside you as you happily pose

for that first photograph, reconciled
to the pain of delivery, beyond it, clean
and alive the pair of you. The records are filed.

The doctors and midwives go. The great unseen
drama is over. I remember it too,
our home birth, your second. Somewhere between

mother and child the blind-spot shows through,
unknown, unseen yet almost locatable, there
and not there, between you and the word 'you'

between the presence in your arms in the air
we all breathe, including the 'me' writing,
this precious, perishable barely remarked affair.

And so in Penig, in the unexpected sighting
of a moment that she, who is at the centre
of this poem yet not there, lost in its low lighting,

would have known as hers, having heard troops enter
and open doors raising the lids of dead eyes
to new light, raising the body that meant her

alone, finding a stretcher from which she might rise
on firm legs, as the official camera rolled
its own myopic eye around, brushing away the flies

so it might blink here on the screen, like an old
dog no longer certain where it is and why,
but is downloaded anywhere, stone-cold.

4 *The Dead*

The stone-cold body that is dressed to lie
along the couch. The stone-cold body dressed
for flames. The stone-cold body in its dry

pod lowered into the ground. The still chest.
The flat hair. The calm statement made
to last. This little life that is compressed

into calendars, into cupped hands, its unplayed
movie locked inside its cells. Where to begin
so the arc of it should rise before it fade

like the rainbow that hovers a few minutes in
the gap between rain and sun, nothing special,
just the usual rainbow, the usual rain, the tin

and copper sound of water falling? To fall
like that is the most natural thing. You raise
your arc, someone observes its brief unofficial

blossoming, utters a few words of praise
then carries on contemplating the arc
of their own being. Here we're in a dead daze.

Here is only Penig, the rainbow gone dark,
all inky greys and blacks, a film's crude
shifts. Once there were girls running in the park,

once there were dates and weddings with fine food,
once there were offices and lifts and beds
that offered sleep like a filmic interlude.

Wrong movie here. Those terrible shaven heads
rise out of a doomed quarry in the last scene
of a discarded reel that the director shreds

as incriminating evidence. What we see on screen
is what remains of it. The arc is chopped
into pieces then spliced together, a vague sheen

of events without detail, everything cropped,
cropped hair, cropped hours, cropped fields and grass. Time
is given short shrift, as if darkness had dropped

on it from a height, crushing it to a single chime.
Ask not for whom it chimes. The extras are paid
in dead coinage, dime by worthless dime.

5 *Excuse*

The past is never the past: it is simply delayed
present. The past is never an excuse. We can
say what we like about the past. We can raid

its archives, find films and texts, select a span
of it, cut and re-cut, splice, add soundtrack;
we can resurrect the voice of woman and man,

slur it, dub it, subtitle, caption it, run it back
so it sounds like prophesy, use it as prologue
or epilogue, render its subtle grey as black

36

or white, says Clio, en passant, in the fog-
bound airport as we're waiting. *Everything's allowed.*
After all it is no crime kicking a dead dog.

I follow her as she cuts through the crowd
hoping to pass her a website address. *Oh that!*
she says on receiving it. *No, I'm not proud*

of that little mess but the dog is dead. The cat
lives on. Nine lives, you know. And so she disappears
into another lounge, like any diplomat,

smooth, brisk and final. *History is skin,*
I tell myself once she has gone. *And she is right*
it's no excuse. But then the films begin

to whirr. Now once again the auditorium light
dips and sinks as if into bone and blood.
Look, there she is now, emerging out of night

into our bedroom. She drags behind her the flood
of herself. She could be anyone, anyone
specific, identifiable. But then her image jud-

ders and freezes. She will remain undone.
Nothing can be completed in her absence.
Nothing can start and nothing can go on.

All we see of the film is present tense.
The past is no excuse. The voice hangs there
like washing left on an electric fence.

Canzone: The Recompense

And then the time came round for the day's fury.
Now finally there would be recompense
and firm apologies for years of fury:
though that was not the way it worked with fury,
not with them. The wind was full of grief
and broke lamenting at the window. Fury
was the tossing of branches. Once the fury
took hold of them they strode about the room
as if there could not ever again be room
for anyone. So either could be a Fury
with hot breath blazing bright in the mouth
as if that was all anyone was: mouth.

They had not thought how fire could burn a mouth.
They came to blows to give shape to the fury:
blows on the arms, across the cheeks, the mouth,
the wind stirring as if air were mouth
and fury itself were somehow recompense
for years of fury. What else could they do but mouth
recriminations at each other to stop the mouth
accusing them. Had they not both known grief?
Is it not natural to cry at moments of grief,
or even years of it? The enormous mouth
of the wind was opening wider while the room
shrank inside its own mouth, hardly a room.

Do not be misled to think this a private room.
It was the room of history. It was the grave mouth
of the dead, the cannon's mouth. Such little room
for even the smallest grief. Even a bedroom
offers a bed where limbs can move in a fury
of delight, but I have known big men room
in tiny rooms, the worse for drink, the room
spinning about them, tightening. What recompense
for them when sober? There was no recompense
for her either, the woman I knew in the last room
of her life. There was no scraping back the grief
to reveal a plain bright room emptied of grief.

38

So things go round, words circle their own grief,
haunting the hallways, moving from room to room
then back again, bumping into the same old grief
in ever narrower spaces, recognising the grief
they thought they'd left behind, an open mouth
forever gaping in astonishment that grief
should always look the same, that worn-out grief
refuses to wear out. And this is cause for fury
and frustration: grief being coupled with fury.
Why not just a clean fury and an end to grief?
That would be reasonable recompense,
if indeed there could be recompense.

And so it is we come to recompense.
The woman in Norman Cameron asks her grief-
stricken lover: *What is this recompense
you'd have from me?* What is due recompense
for time lovers spend in the bedroom?
Nothing compensates: the sea offers no recompense
to the drowned, the drowned no recompense
to those who loved them. Water in the mouth
fills the mouth entirely. Sea and mouth
speak as one. It is all one. The recompense
they looked for was desire for fury
as if to emulate the sea in its fury.

The terrible wind tears curtains in its fury.
The lover looks to press mouth against mouth.
This room is our only room: there is no other room.
What is it branches toss with? Could it be grief?
Could they perhaps be seeking recompense?

IN THE FACE OF HISTORY: IN TIME OF WAR

1 *Atget: Au Tambour*

1

to be literally drumming up custom
to be lost in a doorway
to be free yet in prison
to be marbled barred forbidding *distrait*

to wait for the drumming of rain
for the drumming of the stabled horses we do not see
to be locked in time with nothing but this
to be lost all over again
to be transformed and free

2

come with me to the shelter of the doorway
where there is no rain, where we may kiss
like adolescents in the first throes of romance
as if by chance

let us chalk our names on the blackboard
let us freeze in the cage of the doorway
let us stay here forever or at least today
hearts drumming like cracks on a record

let us walk terrified through the glass
that holds us ragged and will not let us pass

1

Four *poilus* in a wood austerely shitting.
Death watches them, laughing, its sides splitting.

Life is a cry followed by laughter.
The body before, the waste after.

2

Could one hear in that wood the gentle click
of the shutter like the breaking of a stick
or the safety catch on its climacteric?

3

Like the four winds. Like a low fart that rips
clean air in two, like urine that drips.
Four squatting foot soldiers of the Apocalypse.

4

Kiss them lightly, faint breeze in the small leaves,
be the mop on the brow, the sigh that relieves.

Let them dump and move on into the dark plate
of the unexposed future, too little and too late.

3 *Ross: Yellow Star*

The eye is drawn to that single yellow star
that no wise man will follow.
The hunched men in caps, the grimacing woman
her eyes screwed up, cheeks hollow.

We look and look again until we burn a hole
in the paper. We strive to learn
from their resignation but it is beyond us.
We let them burn.

4 *Doisneau: Underground Press*

Were I to fall in love all over again, it would be
with this low ceiling, with the calm faces
of the two men going about their craft
and with her now twisting towards them
beautiful, defiant and free.

Because we forget how beauty was once itself
and nothing else, how it held its stellar
moment in attic and cellar.

Because that is what beauty is, this compact
with time and the silence of concentration
on one subversive operation,

that requires courage and sacrifice
and never comes without a price.

5 *Sudek: Tree*

The visionary moment comes
just as it is raining, just as bombs
are falling, just as atoms

burst like a sneeze in a city park
and enter the dark
as if it were the waiting ark.

You open your hand and blow
the dust. You pick and throw
the stone. You make the round O

of your mouth perfect as light
and the tree bends and stands upright
in the stolid night.

6 Stromholm: Cézanne

Once we were limber and lithe and nubile
we were snakes and fur and dolls and cute,
once we were happening, dreamlike, new-style,
rounded and convolute.

We were brandname and package and sleek as metaphor,
innocent as flesh, mutable as form,
once we were Matisse, and Cézanne and Amadeo, and more,
we went down a storm.

A storm is what descended and always descends,
a sousing, a drowning, a clattering of trays
in the sky to signal miscellaneous ends
to the works of days.

Under the skin, within the bone, in a cell of the nerve
there is laughter, an oddly tickling delight
where the belly tips forward on its precarious curve,
sudden, agonising, bright.

7 Petersen: Kleichen and a Man

I have seen eternity and it is like this,
a man and woman dancing in a bar
in a poor street on an unswept floor.

It clings and plots and is desperate,
at a point between violence and abjection,
between warmth and agoraphobic fear.

Let me reverse this and accept the fear.
Let me drop all objections to abjection,
since life itself is desperate

and has to tread the unswept floor
carefully, lovingly, while the bar
hovers in eternity. Like this.

8 *Kolar: Untitled*

It is less the waiting or the pacing forward,
it is the tree that one leans against, the coarse
bark against the forehead,
the peculiar course

life takes on a day that is suspended
between clock and pulse, that breaks
like splintered
glass or crushed bricks.

Despair is a monument you hardly notice,
an unrecognisable statue in the distance,
a footnote among commentaries
on other destinies.

Then? And then? Nothing. The estate
goes about its business. The bark
comforts or does not.
Lives break or do not break.

9 *Mikhailov: Untitled*

I have seen pietas before where Christ
lies in his mother's lap after the crucifixion.
He does not lie in his mother's lap before the event.
Pieta follows death and nakedness and dereliction.

Young man gazing at me with drugged eyes,
do you aspire to religious ecstasy?
Or are you dead, your thin pale body gone,
beyond fantasy?

Frozen earth. Snow bound fields and nakedness.
Here come the faithful in their woolly hats and gloves,
serving the God that looks you in the face
who records and pities, and – why shouldn't he do so? – loves.

10 *Jonsson: Farmer and gravedigger*

The ladder climbs from the bottom of the grave.
The grave digger stands at the bottom,
a thin elderly man wiping his brow.

We walk the earth feet first, pressing down on it.
Under us move insects and worms.
Whole geological layers shift on a time scale
our feet and hearts cannot measure.

Our tongues try to name us.
Our hands try to hold us.
Our minds to conceive us.

Leaves jostle, grass waves, earth falls away.
Up to our necks in it we keep walking and working
our eyes mouth the spaces between minutes
our skin breathes the air we have no name for.

But we compose elegies and engrave them
on stone, a weightless muttering,
as if we were the universe talking to itself.

11 *Viktor Kolár: Housing estate, 1980*

What you cannot see through those windows
beyond the bare hill
is the hand resting on the table
is the man lying still
on the bed, is the vague gesture
of the young woman in the hallway
as she remembers something that happened yesterday
is the mouse hesitating under the draining board
is the twelve year old boy putting on a record
of *Wiener Blut* that he once saw
his parents waltzing to.

All that you see is the all-but-naked child
on the all-but-naked hill against a naked sky
as if what you could not see were the question
and she the reply.

12 *Henryk Ross: Children of the Ghetto*

Love, we were young once, and ran races
over rough ground in our best shiny shoes,
we kicked at stones, we fell over, pulled faces,

our knees were filthy with our secret places,
with rituals and ranks, with strategy and ruse,
Love, we were young once and ran races

to determine the most rudimentary of graces
such as strength and speed and the ability to bruise.
We kicked at stones, we fell over, pulled faces

and doing so left no permanent traces
because we fought and fell only to confuse
love. We were young. Once we ran races

in ghettos, in camps, in the dismal spaces
of the imagination reserved for Jews.
We kicked at stones, we fell over, pulled faces

at elastic braces, shoelaces, empty packing cases,
as if they were the expressions we could choose.
Love, we were young once and ran races.
We kicked at stones, we fell over, we pulled faces.

However

However you do it, it's done. The wind
rustles the dress. The rain blurs
the face. The morning occurs
in the usual fashion.

However you think, it is thought. The mind
runs on chasing its hare–
brained schemes and the air
continues in motion.

However you hide you are found. The bomb
at the roadside explodes
when it's due to. The secret codes
offer no protection.

However you smile the lips purse. The frown
hovers beside you. It's late,
and the night tells delicate
lies, its stars pure fiction.

Canzone: The Man in the Doorway

It was already late when I passed the doorway,
the time when everyone moves for the exit
and thinks about home. I stopped in the doorway
and looked in. Beyond the open doorway
lay a corridor from which spilled the men
from the office, each one caught in the doorway
for an instant. Was I blocking the doorway?
They did not say so, did not complain. Their gaze
was fixed on the street outside as any gaze
might be. The whole point of a doorway
is to let you through and not to frame a face
you might remember as clear as your own face,

that's in so far as you can know your face,
especially when it appears in a doorway
or in glass, as though it were someone else's face –
and right now it was another person's face.
Perhaps a face must always be in exit,
becoming itself in leaving what is face
behind, as was this office-worker's face.
He had a face, just like the other men
and the look he wore said: *See those other men?*
They are like me, yet this is my own face,
so here I am, drink your fill of it, gaze
at me steadily and meet my own gaze

if only for a second. This is what it is to gaze
at another. This exploring of the other's face
is what we mean when we describe a gaze.
It drains you yet it gives itself. To gaze
is both to drink and be drunk. It is the doorway
to a place you cannot know except as gaze,
the hollow darkness that reflects your gaze
as if it were a voice about to exit
the body, a voice always seeking an exit.
It is your responsibility to gaze
at me, to pick me out among the men
and recognise me, since we are both men.

And indeed we were, the both of us, just men
in a place, though what I gave was not gaze,
not exactly, simply the look that men
give one another, a space where men
meet as men then move on in order to face
responsibilities, the business of being men
as defined by offices, the business of working men:
factory floors, boardrooms, the wide doorway
that gives on to rooms, another room or doorway,
right down to that most basic of rooms marked: MEN
which you will find next to the door marked EXIT.
It is a comedy: half entrance and half exit.

But his face held me. I couldn't simply exit
his gaze as I might that of other men.
It seemed to brood, turn inward, leave no exit
except into itself which is no exit.
The street outside was moving. One might gaze
down it for ever as down some final exit.
I owed him something though, without an exit,
a kind of recognition that his face
had registered, had entered my own face
and would remain there. *Exit! Exit! Exit!*
cried the workers pressing through the doorway.
It seemed that we were really blocking the doorway.

It was our exit. It was our common doorway
into and out of the world we had to face.
He let me go. We disengaged. The gaze
was only itself and we were only men
and everything was sweeping past the exit.

Apropos Palladio

Oh flaking Palladian Palladium
On a backcloth rattled by oom-pah
MARTIN BELL, 'Ode to Groucho'

1

Oh flaking Palladian Palladium! Humble terrace porches!
Banks down the high street, civic halls,
Offices and offices and churches and churches,
Where the great god of money calls
And leaves his deposit like a pigeon!
The portico. The estate. The paradisal region
With its parks and villas,
Its silver trails of caterpillars,
Apiaries, orangeries, conservatories,
And, at the end of the drive, the miraculous ha-ha,
Where a greeting party of rural Tories
Welcomes a rare appearance of The Rajah
Of Surrey in his pantaloons;
Window motifs in the shape of half-moons,
Fantastical topiaries with proper manners
Mumbling in Stephen King undertones,
Elegantly flying banners,
White stones. White bones.

2

Someone down the hall is playing Mozart
To the ticking of a metronome. Keys
Dance under delicate pressure.
Music is proportion you can measure
On a string, with a ruler, but better still
In breath. When it deigns to freeze
It may produce architecture,
A single voice, castrato, the trill
Held at the end of the nose, until
It snaps and lodges in the heart.

3

The imagination can conceive of spaces
The body never inhabits. It dreams in harmonies
Beyond gadgets and furniture: the fridge,
The microwave, the broken chair by the wall.

There is room here for incomplete graces,
For sigh and laughter, for the high ledge
Above the yard, for the child's scrawl
Drifting on a sheet of paper, blown away
In a gust that divides and disposes of families,
For the damp patch creeping gradually
Up the stairwell like a ghost, for
The spot that blossoms like a rosebud
(With just the faintest suggestion of dried blood)
Next to the kitchen door.

4

The imagination is a wonderful invention,
And here's a place it can inhabit
Like an absence which too is something,
Like a sleeve that produces no rabbit,
Like a kind of superhuman humming,
Like a line of pollarded trees,
Like the wind trapped in parentheses,
Like the balance between relaxation and tension.

The imagination is a brilliant coup
With its Apollonian obsessions,
Sums within sums, voice within voice,
Hairline fractures and incisions,
Within which the wee-est mouse
Can harbour grudges and fears
And still not think that all might end in tears,
The walls collapsed and a gale scouting through.

The imagination likes its perfect numbers,
Its Fibonacci series,
Its Modulors, Golden Sections, theories
Involving a soaring staircase and rumours
Of God in the details, in *iambs* and *dactyls*,
The *camera obscura* and perspective
Panning down mean streets, with a private detective
Stalking through the alleys where it slumbers.

5

Come to me, whisper the stones. Spread out your hands
And measure me, I will be conformable.
You can wash yourself in my light.

I am clean as the sky after clouds have passed.
I am a model of the universe in which there are
No black holes, no rogue meteors. My sun
Has no storms, my oceans shift to song
That settles in your educated ears
Like the music of the spheres.

My oceans shift to song. Song is what has been
And what continues whatever the price tag,
Whoever the singer. Clarity of form is clarity
In all and every light. Even clouds have clarity
That comprehends. The meteor has clarity.
The black hole in the mind is a hole in clarity.
Seabirds hang on thermals and hear the clarity
Of the storm. See, I can draw a clear line
Around your hand that washes the world clear.
The eye cleansed by the music of the ear.

The Translators

1

Sometimes you see clouds drifting past the city,
inventions of the sky,
within which images appear then petrify
and remain there in perpetuity.

Otherwise things shift with a certain insouciance
but keep moving. Meaning vanishes
into night, into the vacant parishes
of the imagination, into a non-presence

that is positively terrifying. But there,
the clouds still loom like statues
with faces, as if one could choose
to see them suspended in imagined air.

2

I have jumped to conclusions in my time.
What else would you jump to otherwise?
Look hard into the eyes
of language and you see nothing. Only rhyme

and punctuation. I have talked to ghosts
in ghost language, the solemn dead
at their jabber, hearing the implied instead,
the sigh of the wind at its last post.

I once had a mother who used at times to speak
but now I only conjure her. We carve
images into clouds so we should not starve
for lack of company. We break

the silence into pieces, syllables of space.
We are translated into ourselves. The sky
rushes at us. We observe it insouciantly,
watching clouds move, looking for a face.

3

We have seen mirrors in darkened rooms
hunger for us. We have seen the dead
in our streets. We have felt the dread
of our faces and the shapes a face assumes

in its own mirror. We owe them a shape,
all those faceless one, you and I.
We should feed them before they petrify,
before their clouds pack up or else escape.

4

How do I know myself before I have created
my simulacrum? How are the hungry
to be fed? Listen, the sky is angry.
The gods are demanding to be translated.

NORTHERN AIR – A HUNGARIAN NOVA ZEMBLA

Like words congealed in northern air.
SAMUEL BUTLER, Hudibras

After much perplexity, I found that our words froze in the air before they could reach the ears of the person to whom they were spoken. I was soon confirmed in this conjecture, when, upon the increase of the cold, the whole company grew dumb, or rather deaf; for every man was sensible, as we afterwards found, that he spoke as well as ever; but the sounds no sooner took air, than they were condensed and lost. It was now a miserable spectacle to see us nodding and gaping at one another, every man talking, and no man heard. One might observe a seaman, that could hail a ship at a league distance, beckoning with his hands, straining his lungs, and tearing his throat, but all in vain.

'We continued here three weeks in this dismal plight. At length, upon a turn of wind, the air about us began to thaw. Our cabin was immediately filled with a dry clattering sound, which I afterwards found to be the crackling of consonants that broke above our heads, and were often mixed with a gentle hissing, which I imputed to the letter S, that occurs so frequently in the English tongue. I soon after felt a breeze of whispers rushing by my ear; for those being of a soft and gentle substance, immediately liquefied in the warm wind that blew across our cabin. These were soon followed by syllables and short words, and at length by entire sentences, that melted sooner or later, as they were more or less congealed; so that we now heard everything that had been spoken during the whole three weeks that we had been silent, if I may use that expression. It was now very early in the morning, and yet, to my surprise, I heard somebody say, 'Sir John, it is midnight, and time for the ship's crew to go to bed.' This I knew to be the pilot's voice, and upon recollecting myself, I concluded that he had spoken these words to me some days before, though I could not hear them before the present thaw. My reader will easily imagine how the whole crew was amazed to hear every man talking, and see no man opening his mouth. In the midst of this great surprise we were all in, we heard a volley of oaths and curses, lasting for a long while, and uttered in a very hoarse voice, which I knew belonged to the boatswain, who was a very choleric fellow, and had taken his opportunity of cursing and swearing at me when he thought I could not hear him; for I had several times given him the strappado on that account, as I did not fail to repeat it for these his pious soliloquies when I got him on shipboard.

'Nova Zembla', Journal of Sir John Mandeville, Knight,
quoted by Joseph Addison in *Tatler* No 254 (1710)

NOTE

Sir John Mandeville: The book of travels bearing his name was composed in the 14th century. There are versions in English, Latin and other languages; the original was in French. It was highly popular in the Middle Ages, largely en account of the marvels which it contains. It was not a genuine book of travels, but a compilation out of earlier writers. The author died at Liege in 1372, and was buried in the name of John Mandeville, but this is supposed to have been a fictitious name.

Novaya Zemlya (Russian: 'New Land'; formerly known in English and still in Dutch as **Nova Zembla**) is an archipelago in the Arctic Ocean in the Arkhangelsk Oblast in the north of Russia and the extreme north-east of Europe. Novaya Zemlya consists of two major islands, separated by the narrow Matochkin Strait, and a number of smaller ones. The two main islands are Severny (northern) and Yuzhny (southern). Novaya Zemlya separates the Barents Sea from the Kara Sea. The total area is about 90,650 sq. km.

To set out with no compass but your nose
for the land of certainty and cool judgment,
past moral latitudes, on the back of the wind,
with a plentiful supply of warm clothes
and every spiritual accoutrement
is the dream of the voyager whose mind

seeks resolutions. The train I took was long
as night, as long as memory. It stalled
a little at starting. I looked out at the streets
of the railway suburb and felt strong.
I heard the winter rattling and recalled
the harsh winters, those terrible retreats

in the snow that stripped skin bare, but I
was heading north where everything would
finally be explained, and that gave
me courage to look the north in the eye,
because at the back of it I'd find the good
word, the good that everyone must crave.

The train juddered and we were off again,
the smokers huddled in the rear carriage,
old men at their papers, some women dreaming,
the odd child asleep or crying as if in pain
or out of boredom. As if north were a mirage
we could never reach. As if the land streaming

past the window were illusion. Europe
was our home, but it was an idea of place
that led us northward to its true origin
in the mind. We watched a hill drop
into darkness and I noted my own face
reflected over it, over those virgin

spaces we were now exploring. Had you
been with me then you too would have felt
the excitement. Ice hardened into light.
It was the land of explanations we were coming to,
the clear hard core of things that could never melt
or fade, that grew more brilliant with night.

Oh history, if you could speak the language
of the cold, if you could once head north
into your own frozen heart we might yet
sing from the same song-sheet, lose the baggage
you have made us carry back and forth
and begin, blissfully at last to forget,

because it was the north, however bleak
and strange or even alien to us its cold
might be, there where great whales sunk
and rose beneath the ice cap, I had to seek,
that was the story I wanted to be told,
so I could sleep or dream, or, failing that, get drunk

like all the rest of that northern crew who swarm
across the snowfields, insensible and warm.

2 *Entering Nova Zembla*

In entering the waters of Nova Zembla our words froze
so that however we opened our mouths no sound came,
the world stood still as iced-breath before the nose

like solid cloud, like an amorphous frame
for a lost world where echoes of living speech
might still be found, as if all praise or blame

or intimacy or harshness resided there, and each
of us in our enforced silence might contemplate
the mystery, and hope somehow to breach

some inner law of remembrance, however late,
to find what had been said in the very spot
we left it, our histories, our hearts, the precise date

of their breaking, when they were still hot
in our mouths. But there was terror too
and melancholy, because which of us forgot

the dead we had long stowed and carried through
the journey, the beautiful loved dead, the young
with their rifles and explosives, those who

stood on street corners, the quiet unsung
bodies under the rubble of war crushed
by houses that collapsed like a lung

when the air was sucked out of them, the washed
corpses laid out, the old still queuing for bread,
the leaders hanging in the concrete yard, the rushed

verdicts, the prisons... but what can you do with the dead
except store them in silence, in a cloud of breath
that freezes in front of you? Apprehension, dread,

hope and expectation... history is death
remembered in our country. Childhood is this
frozen cloud, this vanished Nazareth

where we began our progress. We feel the kiss
of that dense impenetrable vapour where
the voice is trapped within its icy ellipsis.

We came to Nova Zembla in good faith. The air
was crisp, the trade routes promising, hull and keel
in order, well-stocked with supplies, with rare

spices to offer potential partners in a deal
of our devising: saffron, chypre, our lives
if necessary. But here we are in our seal

of silence, frozen in, husbands, wives
and children, none of us daring to move.
Is it the voice or the cold air in us that survives

Nova Zembla? That still remains to prove.

3 *Imagining Thaw*

A crackling of consonants that broke above our heads
wrote Mandeville. I hear the crackling of machine-
gun fire, the crump of shells in a street. Our beds

are in the small room where we are in quarantine,
my brother and I. Our consonants ricochet
above our heads, mysterious, unseen

verdicts on the world outside, which is grey
with autumn, shifting into winter. Being ill
we miss the excitement not too far away

from us, right below in fact, in the shrill
whine we cannot explain with the consonants
at our disposal. My parents wait for the radio to fill

the spaces of anxiety. Who are the combatants?
Whose voices crackle at the world like guns?
Our flags of selfhood are tiny, mere pennants

we play with, only our toy soldiers carry weapons.
Out there a new language is being invented,
new *aahs* and *ohs* of grief, new syllabic patterns

out of which grows the peculiar-scented
abstraction of exile, the sour adjectives of defeat
and resentment, for ever *defeated* and *resented*,

and the strangest noun of all, a bitter-sweet
embodiment, somewhere between glory
and triumph embodied in the vast feet

of a statue that has fallen, in the memory
of its falling, and the noise, the terrible noise,
of all those consonants writing their own story.

But then we are nothing more than two small boys
recovering from scarlet fever on the third-floor.
We cannot speak the language that destroys

the city we live in. Later we will learn more
of it. Only later will we grasp its still-raw
grammar and interpret the inchoate roar

of its history. Practice strengthens the jaw
of saying. And soon everything is crackling.
The vowels begin to flow, the consonants thaw.

We live in the north where the sea is not quite cold
enough to freeze the tongue to the roof of the mouth.
Here, the distant crackle of consonants is the *fric*
fric of banknotes, a barely convertible old
currency they only use in run-down places south
of here. Once upon a time before the electronic

wind began to blow, when news was a kind of sighing
in open courtyards, we remembered the sound
of voices that seemed to be stuck in the lift of time forever,
in a neglected tenement where the aged were dying
in rooms with high ceilings and would not be found
by considerate neighbours, or the untidy but clever

graduate on the same floor. We would run upstairs,
there in that southerly country, and make love
on the convertible settee, hearing the world cough
or sing or weep over its rarely mentioned affairs,
aware of the couple noisily talking right above
the bed, or the old woman turning her radio off

next door. What was frozen could remain that way,
like the white noise of the white fridge by the sink,
a vague comfort and nuisance at once. It meant
things were working. And then one extraordinary day
the ice began to melt and the fridge light to blink
and there was a certain agitation in the tenement.

We must learn to talk without allegories and codes.
We must try to make sense of the unexpected thaw.
The dead in the fridge have begun to sing
in a language we might understand, the roads
have been gritted. The traffic moves to the law
of traffic. There must be a time for everything.

Perhaps the weather has broken in Nova Zembla.
Perhaps the consonants now crackling will inform
the vowels they have been sleeping with. Perhaps
the punctuation of guns and breath resemble
each other more than we think, and the storm
of voices in the radio, those wheezes, taps,

knockings and screechings are ready to create
a past we can live with. Nineteen fifty-six.
A journey of half a century. A whole childhood
spent on a leaky vessel with a lying captain and mate.
Old names are subject to a changing physics.
A Cape of Hope somewhere is reckoned Good.

SONGS OF THE WRESTLER JOZSEF SZABO

1 *Rabbit, 1944*

I was a rabbit first, and now am one again.

Back in the darkness, when the bombs began
To fall and the roof caught fire, we ran
Into the yard in our nightclothes
And hunkered down in a ditch as the outhouse rose
Into the air and black ash swirled like crows.
                We lay and watched fire rage
About our small domain, the rabbit cage
On the far side so we couldn't see the damage,
But when it was all over and we were alone
With the smell of roasting flesh, the rabbits were gone,
Just hanks of fur and blackened shards of bone.

                        It was morning and the dew
Shook on the grass among the cinders. Dust flew
Into our eyes as the cold wind blew
The house clean. I too shook like a rabbit, my eyes
As red as the angoras' unsettling cerise
In a mist of snow. I seemed to hear their cries
And saw them turn and quiver, cocking their ears,
Some whistling, others screaming against the spears
Of light that skewered them. I saw their tears
In the dew, watched them turn to blood
Leaking into puddles in soft mud,
Small beads, each a tiny rosebud.

My brothers and I shouted and fought
In the sunlight as if we had caught
Some rare disease, a twitch, a thought
As furred as a hairball, a flying germ
With claws that made us tremble and squirm
As we beat each other until we were firm
Flesh once more, until our mother called
From the doorway of the house and we crawled
Away and stood up, as if time itself had stalled
And held us frozen.

                    Those rabbits were almost
As old as I was and now they were all lost.
I saw a shrub shake as if a rabbit ghost
Were nibbling at its foot among nettles and dock
And the white scut of a dandelion clock
That I bent down to pluck
And blow away as we ourselves were blown.

So we go floating, each of us alone,
Our endings and our whereabouts unknown.

Back then I was not minded of such things.
My mother called again. I left the petal wings
To their windblown scuttlings
And returned to breakfast, to what remained downstairs:
A blackened table, a few broken chairs,
And carried on calmly with our own affairs.

2 *London, 1959*

Land of green hills and fog and a sour dull sea
Banging its head against concrete, offering free
Gifts of clothes and employment, how we
Loved you even as we puzzled out your ways
Trying to pick through your language, through days
Exactly like each other in off-season chalets
Down promenades and piers among pools of beer
And windblown papers. How we wondered at your queer
Notions of amusement, your Christmassy cheer,
Your drill halls, your cliff paths, your pubs, your cold
damp sheets and grey blankets, your caddies and cups
and cosies, your digestive biscuits, your shops
brimming with bargains, your boiled sweets and pear-drops,
the sheer tastelessness of your dinners. We became
your walking clichés, playing the game
of foreigners with souls. We laid claim
to your manners. We filtered through into your short
afternoons, your six o'clock news, into the sport
you watched on your tellies. It was a superhuman effort
entering your houses with their two up two down
stairways, your suburbs, your overspill new town
terraces, your slums, locating something we could own.

Now here we are, hanging by a thread
fed out by Fate, dangling, assimilated, accepted,
lodged. Here I lie too. Here I can lay my head.

3 *József in the Mirror, 1965*

When I consider my body I see it hold
space in a ring. I sense the controlled
Energy of my arms. I note the concentrated cold
Eye as it weighs its options, the tense but light
Sway of the hip. I am all appetite
And readiness for advance or flight.
I feel the mechanism of the muscles, the click
Into place of the bone, am aware of the tick tick
Of the heart, of blood's hoarse music
In the ears. I can hear my temples boom
Instructions to my limbs as they seek room
In ambient air. My eyes widen. My lungs bloom
And expand into formal gardens. My spine
Holds firm as a tower or a pillar down a mine.
My fingers extend and bend to the design
Of my maker who is alert to my neural needs.
My forehead is wide. I don't mind if it bleeds
Under razors or blows, whatever best feeds
The world's bloodlust. I observe through the mask
Of my own face the masks of others who ask
questions I must answer. It is my pleasant task
to help them answer the ones I put to them for
ever. My bruises and fractures keep the score
of my victories. My very hips are a metaphor
for the cradle that rocks us both. They are the seat
of my shadow, the crumpled, concrete
evidence I support on two firmly planted feet.

4 *Ditch, 1972*

I am the masked man, the Zorro of London, but my face
Is uncovered each night in the mirror in the space
Behind my eyes where wild rabbits chase
Each other across the field and I am alone
At the side of a ditch of stagnant water overgrown

By dock and nettle and rubbish thrown
Still floating in the thickness on dull green
And brown squabs decomposing in a sheen
Of unearthly light and the odd soaked magazine
Some adolescent has left behind full of bare
Flesh now smelling of nothing but stale air
Much like my own body and its coarse grey hair.

If I could tell you everything in the clearest terms
I would do so but somehow language squirms
Through my fingers like maggots or worms
In the slime of telling what I am not
And never could be, part of a comprehensible plot
Or even a story that did nothing but run on the spot,
Because this is the spot I have run on and only time
Has slithered beyond me through the slime
Of telling, and this awkward rhyme
Leaves me standing at the side of a ditch
Of dredge water, telling me look: this is the rich
Soil you spring from, the soil into which
You'll vanish, there's no disgrace in it,
Since all kinds of creatures find their place in it
And you too may dip your bare face in it.

5 *Big Daddy, 1978*

From the start it was Big Daddy and I, way back
In the darkness where he stood, belly-slack
Bending my arm behind me so I could hear it crack.
He was there in the boarding house by the sea
Where we fetched up, in the cup of milky tea
On the lace doily, in the broken-toothed key
They lent us for late nights. He was there in the gym
In my childhood where I was afraid of him,
And even them he was never exactly slim-jim
Or svelte but barrel-chested, almost squat
With a potentially enormous gut
When he told us to stretch and keep out mouths shut,
There from the beginning as Big Daddies are
Though just as often they're propping up the bar
Or belching and winking but never very far
And you wonder how they carry that slab

Of grease about so easy to grab
And twist in your fingers, that gives as you jab
And avoid his rough lunge, which is a skill
You learn early if you learn it at all: that still
Moment before you spill
From the ring or skip aside as in a dance
Where the floor is on fire, taking your chance,
While the heavier man loses his balance.
Oh the beauties of wrestling: I could tell
You of such devices the very smell
Of them would drive you crazy, that hell
Itself could not have dreamed their names;
I see them barely contained by the white frames
They burst from like hot air, in flames.

Shining Jack

A man who thinks too much and feels too little
STEPHEN KING

I have known and been with them, those men
who think too much and feel too little.
They feel nothing. The terrible hours vanish.
They wake to an ordinary morning. They rattle
about one vast accommodating mind
until sensation itself seems to diminish
to a trace that can barely be defined.

I think of Jack Nicholson busting a gut
in the manic bar: *Twisted Jack, Violent Jack,
Jack Horror, Jack Dull-Boy, Jack Pure-Evil,
Possessed Jack*, who watches the camera track
through an empty hotel he cannot properly feel
only think and think and see again: the shut
doors, the restaurants, the ghosts, unreal
figures of thought moving through primeval
spaces, scene after scene after scene,
leaving no trail, the whole place pristine.

Can he feel a thought coming? Is it there
on the soundtrack? Does it whet its axe-blade
in some outbuilding on a furious grindstone?
*Hello. Are you there? And if so, are you alone?
What if a thought billows through you in the cold air?
Are your defences in order? Are you afraid?*
I think that's what they're thinking when they touch
their own faces. Not much to feel there. Never very much.

Canzone: On Dancing
(for Helen)

The tightrope dancer shimmies between two cliffs
as if it were not death waiting below
but the bed he left that morning, as if cliffs
were stations of sleep. Dancing between cliffs
is his business. So language too must dance
over a void between the figured cliffs
of meaning and nonsense, the rift between two cliffs
spanned by rope that trembles like a string
of the guitar when plucked. A piece of string
will do: a line, a sentence, both require cliffs,
a fall, a breath, and the skip of feet along
a rope that always seems too long.

It's there because it is natural to long
for the other side, the distance between cliffs
being the sum of longing. That's why we long
for cliffs and distances. And life's not long
when seen from cliff-height. The rocks below
take seconds to reach. We seem to belong
to them, sometimes we almost long
for those rocks, that fall. That is why we dance
not walk, because the spirit of dance
is superfluity, capering long
and short as it strides, so we strike the string
and make music precisely by stopping string.

One woman timed her days with string.
She felt them tighten. Her life had been too long
tied up in one inefficient heartstring.
Her body was thin by the end, a piece of string
fraying between the barren cliffs
of then and now. She knew too much of string
and its vibration. She had no wish to string
days out. She had walked in landscapes below
the cliff and climbed to the top. What lay below
was music that could not be played on a string
between cliffs. She heard the tune they dance
to underneath, knew the steps of that dance.

But that is the fascination of dance
above a place of fall. The string
makes music; its length and height the only dance
in our power. Never lords of dance
merely dancers whose time is only as long
as a piece of string, we move to the dance
we hear in our heads or interpret as dance.
Of course we know they're figurative cliffs
(hence we make figures) yet they're real as cliffs.
We sense the height and turn it into dance.
We breathe the air, those years of space below,
Dizzy with concepts such as *above / below*.

A train at the local station. Footnotes below
a small timetable. Posters advertising a dance
at the village hall: forms of life below
the line. A lost shoe or glove just below
the multi-storey car park is the end of a string
of coincidences. Grab it. Nothing is below
us here. Even our highest notes are low
compared to those we imagine, for which we long
and seem to hear. The street is where we belong.
We are simply people who walk below
High buildings that loom above us like cliffs.
Cliffs are like that. We dance between such cliffs

to songs echoing between two cliffs.
There is nothing more natural for us than to long
for the perfect dance step along the taut string
whose music is stopped vibration. *Let's dance*,
sings the singer to the echo a long way below.

The Storyteller

Two of Four Houses

The first spoke. What I see is a house, or the idea of a house, enormous and unknowable in its full extent, a house in which rooms only partly reveal themselves, in which mirrors are to be walked into, pictures disappeared into, in which chairs and beds are big enough to swallow you entirely. I can never see any part of this house, not one room, not one corridor clearly, only as a patchwork of dark and light (chiefly dark) containing isolated angles of objects or furniture. Its smell however is overpowering, and it has a music too, comprised of creaks, whispers and snuffles; rain on glass, branches on windows, someone yawning, someone singing in a kitchen, someone listening to a radio in a distant room, a music always elsewhere. There are rooms here with walls so damp you are guaranteed to get rheumatism, and floors so rotten it is dangerous to step on them. In the dark there are rusty old tins waiting to cut you. Some rooms are so filled with hatred you can smell it across a stairway. I couldn't begin to number the attics and cellars; the pantries, privies and vaults; the kitchens are far below. There is no outside to this house. Nature is purely notional – a breeze that blows in through an open window, books that show men clinging to precipices or rafts, buckled across wires or lying in pits. Every so often a shudder passes through the fabric: the house is bending with some erotic dream. You touch your flesh and you know it is distended. You taste salt. Here and there you might glimpse couples huddling together, holding hands or shouting hoarsely at each other. You might see one cradling the head of the other, feeling a pulse, passing from a room carrying a bedpan or a towel.

The second followed. The house I want to tell you about is much smaller and much more specific. I have only seen it once but know about it through my mother who lived there. The first thing you should know is that it overlooks a park with a skating rink in it. The skating rink lies over the road and the house itself is built into a hillside. It is therefore possible to stand at one of the upper windows, or on the narrow wooden balcony running along the top storey and see through the bare trees of the park directly to the pond which was always frozen over in the winter. From the house the figures on the pond would appear small of course, scarcely distinguishable from each other, but if they knew you were there, watching them (a single figure at a window or on a balcony, especially a figure expected to be there, is much more likely to be identified) they would sometimes turn to you and wave broadly, with exaggerated gestures, maybe because they knew you well or thought well of you, or because they simply wanted to be amusing, to amuse you in particular and their friends in general. Waving from the pond must have been a consciously significant gesture. From the window or balcony you could follow the line of trees leading away from the pond towards the frozen bandstand, lit by a small lamp post (who knows who you might see there, they didn't wave), and beyond it, past the transverse ditches to the street at the end (hardly visible) where you knew you would find the theatre. So theatre, bandstand and pond would form a triad from the window and this was the park's attraction. You think of this house as something to look out of rather than live in. Living in it proved uncomfortable, almost disastrous, for the part where the house lay below ground was damper than it first seemed when the house was bought one summer. The smell of damp emerged only slowly in the late autumn, but it persisted and intensified throughout the winter, well into March. Then smell gave way to an aroma, a drift of lilac and honeysuckle but by the summer the only smell remaining was the gentle burning of cushions left too long by open windows in the blistering heat, and perhaps a distant and discreet odour of excrement from heaven knows where. If the house had a peculiar magic it was only because all old houses have it, especially in strongly contrasting or moving light: in summer dark splinters crannied among the bright slabs; in spring and early autumn the thin shifting patterns as clouds are driven across the window or boughs twitch or buck in the wind, and in winter in the movements of gas- and fire-light.

And then came the third.

And the fourth.

A Hermit Crab

As people age and die something in them hardens and yearns for survival. It is the ego seeking to ward off completion. Look at the faces. The bones emerge, the nose juts, the cheekbones drop into angles. This is the ego emerging, stating its hard and impossible conditions to time, who is certainly not going to listen. Nevertheless, one man tells jokes till he bursts, another reads aloud to his friends, the words settling in the folds of his skin and clothes. Both men hear their words and feel assured, if only for as long as they continue talking, that they are still the active element in their lives. The rock shapes the wind. The rock emerges from beneath the flesh. But the spirit? Moss on the rock, oil in the water, a kind of deposit like salt. I watched a hermit crab scuttling in a pool at Holkham. It assured me to fit the words 'hermit crab' to this tiny particle stumbling to and fro. In the beginning was the Word. The word scuttles to and fro. Language solidifies and emerges from the waves.

The Hands

Her movement had an exaggerated grace, a flamboyance that was poetry and gross hyperbole at once. It was the same with her handwriting. She held the pen high up the barrel and waved her wrist about, whipping each word into at least one unwonted flourish. Even now, as she stood in the dock, the hands were arching and flourishing, out of control, straying to her forehead, plucking at her hair, pinching and twisting her jumper. And still it tantalised.

Perhaps that was the problem. Perhaps it was herself she tantalised. There was every reason for this. Both her intelligence and her beauty had the same wild, ragged edge. She was vulnerable, and who can resist that? Not the magistrates sitting at their bench. Not the rougher deities of Holloway prison. Not all the mothers of the world in their professorial chairs in the wailing universe.

And the hands had their own life entirely. They were never prisoner's hands, but hands all by themselves, in their own circle of air, the circle they were just now describing so flamboyantly.

The Memory Man

The touch of other people's fingers is perhaps the most intimate of contacts when solicited: to sit at a table and touch fingertips with the person opposite may be to recreate the spark of creation, it has such an exploratory mutuality about it, focusing, as it does, the whole nervous system into five points of concentration. Magician utters spells into magician: self rides on skin, fingertips develop Velcro surfaces, part velvet part fur, cats leap from fingers in a shock of adrenalin.

Since my first memories are of living in a street whose name may be translated as 'gardener street' I will call my detective Gardner. His shadow, his fellow prisoner, will call himself Gardiner – the name as misspelt on an official looking brown envelope in his jacket pocket – though we cannot know whether that is his real name. Gardner begins to wriggle his fingers under the biting rope and touches the shadow's right middle finger. He is naturally startled. At first he cannot tell whether the finger is that of a man or a woman but the shock makes him freeze. He becomes aware of the other's breathing, his warmth, his voice saying something, telling him to push, to push away. Where are they? In Gardener Street of course, though they do not know this. Gardner pushes with all his might. The shadow pushes. There is a door in front of Gardner, a tall dark brown affair in a simple dark brown case. He doesn't know what is behind him. They wriggle in their seats, make counter movements, push, pull, get the rope to rub against the chair backs. Slowly it begins to loosen, now they can rock away from each other, now their ankles find an inch or two to kick in, their elbows work free, they are afraid of toppling. As their shoulders move forward they are like a bud opening, a heady blossom unfurling on a floral carpet into the smell of furniture polish and the sound of a piano downstairs, on a radio. Now Gardner has an arm clear of the ropes and is busily undoing the rest. He kicks like a baby, cuts himself here and there, and finally does topple forward, painlessly, against a settee with its soft upholstery, free at last.

This is the easy part, I tell her. I can envisage the room, the door, the carpet and the settee. I can furnish the place, no problem. I can smell it, move through it, turn its noises on or off, adjust the volume control, swivel my eyes left or right. It is after all only virtual reality, a room in the head. All rooms are rooms in the head, she replies, even real rooms, but I can see she's interested. Well, presumably she could turn me on or off, adjust my volume, get up now and walk away. Only, I plead, there are real things with real distances between them. Too theoretical, she answers. Precisely, I retort. How far have I distanced you already, I think regretfully, how deep below the story lies the real story? Where, in this high hall with its high music, does tangible life begin?

Is Gardiner good or evil when he tells Gardner about his father? Tells him that his dad was a slim short man with a careworn face, that he smelled of tobacco and old women? Is it good to know that he, the father, was a furtive boy sliding between aunts, listening to old men with white beards and bad breath dying in over-decorated, over-stuffed rooms; that Gardner himself only remembers this because at some moment it became clear to him in a conversation, and crystallised if only for a moment and for ever. He could tell Gardner anything. A naked boy is cowering under a table, he says, he feels the air on his skin, especially the parts usually unexposed and this feels good, because under the table he can see socks and shoes and ankles moving away from him into worlds of their own, leaving him alone with the air and his hands on the carpet. He tells Gardner what was written on his third year school report, who cornered him in the playground in the junior school and punched him, describes his nose bleeding. He could be making it up, of course. You make it up. It is not what happened but the fact that the shadow seems to know it that is of consequence. I think it is best that you should sense a touch of evil about Gardiner. You should suspect his motives. It is, after all, suspicious. Who would go to such trouble to find out about you? Do you like it? I ask her.

She likes the evil. Everyone does. Gardiner is certainly malevolent. But what can he want? What is the plot? Why be a shadow and attach yourself to someone in this way?

You have to feel the natural proportions of the enigma, play it out at full length.

I tell her that when I look out of my window every morning I see the same bicycle leaning against a lamp post. It has a lot of plastic bags hanging from the saddle and handlebars. It is like a pale, milky, distended bunch of grapes, ballast to hold a life down. That bicycle is a life but I rarely see the life it belongs to. It arrives early and leaves sometime in the afternoon when I'm not looking. It is an object of frustrated fertility, a symbol parked right outside my door with a real man on it, moving, on what, from here, seems to be a pathetic daily circuit. I could go out and touch the bags or push the bicycle over. I too could be malevolent. But why start a chain of events I know nothing about?

Pisanello

The mechanical revolution will be an elegant, aristocratic affair. Our very oil will be descended from blue-veined deposits. Our fuel will be ideas bred at high altitudes.

From the yo-yo, to the hawser, to the wind-up watch on our wrists, our tensions will be calibrated to a nano-technological standard. We will invent the uplift bra and a device for producing heavy water. The micro-circuitry of sonnets and the horse-power of the spring-loaded mousetrap will advertise our capabilities to the stars, which have hitherto been deaf, but which, henceforth, will hear us down long invisible tubes, antennae and rotating discs. When we doff our hats there will be decapitations. When we take a deep breath bodies will be defenestrated from the windows of Central European public buildings.

War will be aesthetic. Blood will spout in blade-thin arcs across fields measured by pulsions. Under the fields the bones of the dead will knit like pieces of living Meccano. The clicking-noise you hear is the bones conspiring. The grass is singing madrigals. Cavalcanti and Dante go walking through the wood of suicides.

A HOWARD HODGKIN SUITE

Howard Hodgkin Considers Realism

In autumn I go to Venice where I lose
all sense of direction among the canals.
Returning with damp socks and leaky shoes,
I lie down in the hotel, gaze at the walls.

No sense of direction. Not just canals
but alleyways and vacancies and yards;
hotels where salesmen lie and gaze at walls
thinking of autumn, shuffling business cards.

More alleyways, more vacancies, more yards!
For Rimbauds of vacancy, regret, faint brown
autumnal banknotes, packs of business cards,
Venice is where autumn comes to drown.

So where's romance? or vacancy? the faint brown
uniform of regret that leaves trees bare?
Venice is where autumn comes to drown
its sorrows, a business foreclosing, an affair.

Regret is uniform. The trees are bare.
Here is where we should live, if we could choose.
The business of sorrow forecloses the affair.
In autumn I go to Venice where I lose.

Howard Hodgkin Considers the Moon

When it comes to me, green, through the green window
it is not green but brown. When it enters the back
of the eyes it is not brown but black with a faint afterglow.
When I wake in the night, once again it is black,
then swells into a kind of gold or foxed yellow.

When the moon rises, that which is cold freezes
and creeps under the nails with a peculiar noise
I can't quite identify. When, eventually, it squeezes
through the double glazing it is a blend of alloys
passing through the usual predictable phases:

now full, then mildly dented like an old football,
cut sharp in the middle, a slice of lemon,
the merest sliver of ice left on the floor, a small
dense patch of nothing. But who are these women
sitting immobile, patient in the hall?

I feel their cold. Their manners are the *politesse*
of death, their small talk is of moons waning.
I watch them as they rise and dress
in little black numbers. Their stars hang
in the cupboard. The moon waits on the terrace.

Howard Hodgkin Considers Lunch

Let's lunch under striped awnings. Let there
be clean tables and a view of the bay
where nothing moves, only the light
before the distant end of day
and a slight movement of cool air
to foreshadow night.

Let it be orderly as clothes in a trunk
just opened. Let there be fresh salad
and cheese and bottles of fine wine.
Let there be arms, bodies of solid
flesh. Let's get mildly drunk.
Let the last word be mine.

Let's vanish as though we never were.
Let the bed not show any trace
of those who have slept there or moved
the pillows or rubbed their face
in the sheets. Let the wind stir
the curtains, unfelt, unloved.

Howard Hodgkin Considers a Small Thing But His Own

Darkness frames small things, so I rejoice
in spluttering some colour into life.
Do I stay in bed and mope, lament my choice

of partner or pigment? Not my style.
See, if I cup this hand the light shines through it
and no amount of moping will undo it.

Or so I say to myself last thing at night
when it is dark, as the blackest dog despair
can find, sheds her silky hair

pretty well everywhere.

Three Pontormos for Peter Porter

1 *Visitation: The Burning Mothers*

If only, she said, we could be born of fire
as well as die in it, if only our mothers
could be called to be flames, or be eaten
by flames and be ash like all those others;
if just once the flames could be beaten
down that burn us from within
so that we ourselves might finally retire...

I watch them flickering into life, their gowns
blown this way and that, with each child
about to be born into light and those faces
impassive as the logs that must be piled
on to keep them burning: savage graces
for ever under the bright skin,
billowing fires of burning towns.

2 *Supper at Emmaus: An Empty Plate*

The plate will be empty off which they must feast.
The eye of God will sort out man from beast.
The grace of God will change the nature of bread.
Wine will be blood as soon as the Son is dead.
The grace of God exists that grace might be
Lodged somewhere in creation: *gratis*, free.

Here it's the wind that dominates. You'll note
those somewhat surprising colours. I combine
them against expectation, so red, for instance,
in the form of pink, is darker than yellow
in the form of orange. As for the blue, that sozzled
rain-dark pastel blue that seems to float
between tones so the whole thing's shrill
or gives an impression of shrillness, a dance
expressive of frenzy if you like, that billow,
that settlement of blue-grey you couldn't quite define
as blue of any one sort but leaves pink dazzled,
that's what the rest sink into or settle on,
while at the bottom the luminous figure of John,
the beloved disciple, glows, squat and still,
so light on his feet you'd not think he supports
the death of God and the wind that blows
the world awry and away so everything flows
towards a grace that elevates what it distorts.

Canzone: A Film in January

(for Clarissa)

When light is a vague film that seems to rest
on the surface of the eye like a weight
you barely feel or register, you may rest
assured it is January. Time to arrest
time, since nothing moves, only a few leaves
shuddering in a draught. As for the rest,
it is expectation of what might follow rest
as naturally as day, or what amounts to day,
follows the thicker dark now that all day
is given over to slenderness and unrest,
now that we drift about in a winter film,
two shadow characters on shadow film

who are sure to discover that their part in the film
has been edited down to a single January, the rest
discarded along with years of light and film;
that, out in the street, traffic is a film
of movement without moment or weight,
its ghosts never given credit on a film
though film couldn't do without them. Ghosts and film
are of one substance. World arrives and leaves
without so much as a stirring of dead leaves.
But that's not life, you say, that's merely film
and film is different from life. Meanwhile day
goes on with the business of being day

never isolated from the traffic of day
where no high street is mere film-show. *If you want film
go to a cinema*, it says. The old at midday
shelter in shop-fronts to watch the short day
pass before hunkering down to their afternoon rest.
Soon evening drifts down light as film. Today,
for them, like all winter days, is a thin day.
For them the body is a lifetime's weight
that has to be carried about as dead weight
nor can film lighten it, not by a single day.
They are all-but-unreadable leaves
of haunted books, not those dead leaves

you see swept along the pavement. Each one leaves
a ghost image on the unexposed day
until the camera crew ups and leaves
for another location. Cinematic leaves
fly off the calendar, it being that kind of film,
that kind of life. Language interleaves
what life abandons when, inevitably, it leaves
its ghosts behind, since language is never at rest.
Your language, my language. Nothing can rest
easy in the knowledge of it. The word leaves
the mouth it stews in, flitters about weight-
less but capable of stinging. It gains weight

only by repetition. And so the weight
of years in our open mouths gathers and leaves
us gasping. Love is too serious a weight
to be speaking of lightly. An underweight
string of words vanishes in the cold light of day,
in January especially. It is body-weight,
heart-weight, metaphor-weight, the word 'weight'
I weigh here. Our lives are rushes of film
that must carry the weight of the world on film,
on high street, on works of days, in the weight
of an imagined library of lives that won't rest
however we speak them. There is no point of rest:

nor is that exactly what we want, not rest,
only the stillness found on a single frame of film
with just enough love to get us through cold day.
Is love what remains of us? Is that what time leaves?
Is that the statue? Is love that dense grave weight?

The Birds

Set the clock going

Time shrinks back into itself, curls up small,
Until it's no more than a newly-born
Child or a fieldmouse scurrying past a wall

Of the house where the child lies. Time shorn
Of its fur, of its history, is not time
But absence, something you can shoe-horn

Into any space. It is the romantic sublime
Waiting for us in bed with days on its hands,
With history, change, the regular chime

Of the body-clock, the rustling sands
Of the human hourglass with its nipped waist,
The breathless waiting for a moment that stands

As still as the furniture so carefully placed
For human convenience, into which room
Human concerns file with their curious chaste

Demands such as: *Love me. Do not assume*
Authority over me. Try to be a comfort.
Feed me. Empower me. Bring me to bloom,

Now! Life is virginal at core and short,
The ego unbroken, forever folded in
Upon itself, the refuge of last resort.

Difficult then for anyone to begin
A conversation with love or to start
Anywhere but with the delicate thin

Light of the room, the tender colour chart
Of the child's face, the frail shell of the voice
Within which it moves, the thrum of the heart

In its barely opaque chest. It's best to rejoice
In what arises, since delight as simple as this
Is singular and never spoilt for choice.

Mind the Door

No shortage of the romantic sublime. It drops
About your head in bomb-showers, flowering
Into fire. It flashes across your scalp and crops

Mountains to leave the ashen dead cowering
In burned-out ditches. It careers across the road
In large goods vehicles, rises in towering

Buildings, up lift-shafts, reads the genetic code
Of suffering and cracks it like matchwood, the *me*
And *you* of it gone. It is happy to explode

Itself then come back for more. It whips the sea
Up like stiff cream and shatters it like glass
Then spills it into the shallow sanctuary

Where the poor have gathered waiting for it to pass.
The child's bed is a speck of dust it notes
In its passage across a million blades of grass,

One of several million other such motes
Of light it sweeps by, lonely, magnificent,
Meaningless as it calms down and floats

Away serenely with its energy unspent.
The same with history whose headlong rush
Excuses the odd unfortunate event

Preferring power, the work of the broad brush,
To responsibility with its insistence
On clean laundry and a regular wash.

History's inches are icons of long distance,
Its ideas best realised at heights
Requiring neither comment nor assistance

From those citing individual rights
As their excuse. The child lies in its bed
Watching light shift while days and nights

Succeed each other, wholly unassisted.
Desire begins and loss. Music swells
Behind the closed door where the elders tread.

The Girl in the Dressing-gown

A girl in a dressing gown, about nine years old,
Turns towards the camera and smiles back
At the photographer. It is the controlled

Moment. It is Vermeer and Goya, the crack
Between great landmasses of becoming,
Almost an elsewhere, the point where the track

Becomes visible as it vanishes, numbing
And quickening. You can see the earlier face
And read the later one. Time keeps drumming

Its fingers impatient with being in one place
So long, but here it is now. Look. Just there
In the flash of the eye, in the faint trace

Of foreknowledge we detect and seem to share
With her like hindsight or a guess
We must hazard because chance is everywhere.

Slowly the word 'you' begins to address
Her condition. *You*: the camera's trick
Of intimacy and numb tenderness.

So let us say *you* to her. *You*, says the click
Of recognition. Yes that was the girl
With the pearl ear-ring, the aristocratic

Maya, the startled bride in Chagall's whirl–
Wind orbiting the moon. But this is merely
Conversation between images that unfurl

Like flags to mark the spot where *you* nearly
Stand at age nine, the future drawn towards you
Determined never to see you as clearly

As the present can. Something is travelling through
The grey veins of the grey print. I daren't name it
Because naming is too easy. Naming is what we do

When taking possession. We call it and so claim it,
But the moment is unclaimed. The image is elsewhere
Let somebody else develop it and frame it.

Naming

That *you* swims out of incomprehensible
Water, a local stream bearing shopping bags,
Old shoes, dead leaves, petals, past a scribble

Of froth caught on the bank where the tide drags
Past low branches according to its own
Genetic code, a hieroglyph all swags

And flourishes, the flowing and the flown
Merging into each other. Who can read
A language so mumbled, in such undertone?

Threadbare capillaries tangle and bleed
Under the skin of it. *I'll tell you who you are*
Says the bully. *You are the narrow weed*

I can twist round my finger. You are the avatar
Of terminal weakness. I name you mine
And dispose of you. I can throw you as far

As a body can fly. Beyond the thin grey line
Of the stream, on the far bank, behind a wall
That shelters a garden, in its own crystalline

Moment, the self hears the distant call
Of the voice that must find it, that knows its shape
From within, but is not quite locatable

Either in the head or in the singular landscape
They both inhabit. The landscape is all echo
And distance. It is impossible to escape

From it and see it whole. So you, my love, know
No more than I do where we stand and hear
Each other call by name whatever names shadow

In voices that waken, comfort and endear
Themselves to us through their brokenness
And make a piercing sweet cry in the ear.

Dressing

Out of the dark a torso, more garment than flesh,
The weight of invisible breasts behind the high
Empire line and twist of cord; empty and fresh

As air. It is just waiting for you to try
The outfit on for size, to become woman
And fill it out without pondering the why

And how of it, to step into the common
Form-hugging sheath and gracefully undertake
The obligations implied by such things. No one

Goes naked in the world after all. For whose sake
Do you become who you are? Are you alone
In the dark? Is it for yourself you ache

In the morning? Even if you were stone,
Like this goddess, you would desire beyond
Your fixity something already half-known

Yet negotiable. As a child you respond
To the adult's gravity with a blank stare
Of instinctive hunger. You touch your blonde

Hair and bunch it in your fist. You prepare
Your flirtatious look. You play at control,
Then lost, start crying at the small despair

You're stuck with. But this is the soul
Prepared for you, these garments that glow
In the dark and burn as fierce as coal.

And out of the same dark step the slow
Suitors in their allotted garments, unsure
Of their own identities, hoping to follow

The patterns they've guessed at, a mature
Untroubled roundness weighing at their hearts,
And the breasts press against cloth as if nature

Insisted they do so, as if there were darts
Piercing them, as if becoming were all
In the hollow waiting garment that closes and parts.

Kindertransport

As a child you move slowly over the vast
Floor of the kitchen, the almost endless yard,
Crawling over both while minutes crawl past

In the opposite direction. Once you discard
The walking frame you hurtle between handholds
Of chairs and cupboards, taking the odd hard

Knock, while your anxious mother comforts and scolds
In equal measure. But your world is still small
As you discover in the car as one hill folds

Into another or an older child climbs the high wall
That hides the desirable, barely imagined domain
Of elsewhere that is located beyond parental

Granting. The world expands but will never deign
To offer itself whole, you quickly realise,
Nor does it feel any obligation to explain

Its motives. But what if, before your very eyes,
Things change, flip over, vanish or explode?
It happens sometimes. Alien empires rise

Like towers, thousands scatter down the road.
As a child you move with them unmoved, quaint,
Adaptable, curious, carrying your tiny load

Of responsibility. Girl and boy. The faint
Lines of gender wash briefly away in the haste
Of departure without a word of complaint

In the great gust wafting you onward. Why waste
Time on difference when the powerful cohesive
Of fear holds the clock together and the displaced

Are in one small corner or container? We live
From moment to moment, say the sharpened senses
Working through ears and eyes, say the plaintive

Cries of those left behind. We are without defences,
Without options. It's where we go. It's where
We are. And here we are, clambering over fences,

Entering the given space others prepare
For us, we children, we romantics, we fallers
In love in gardens, with our fistfuls of hair.

Once upon...

Once upon a time the story was told
Of a time before time, an unfixed point in space
We could inhabit while the adult world rolled

Past us, a story in which the desperate race
Was internalised in the drumming sound
Of pulses, settling forever behind the face

We made at the precise moment we found
The hidden treasure, the lost child, the frog
Turned prince, the giant or genie unbound

And risen, the terrifying saucer-eyed dog,
The witch with the metal nose, the very image
Of Tycho Brahe found years later. Our dialogue

Was with creatures requiring kindness and courage.
We were not ourselves as seen in the looking glass,
Not firmly definable, but a kind of mirage

That attended and haunted the back of the class
When the teacher's voice blurred into afternoon
And the sun had long slipped by under the grass

And the distant houses were gone or would be soon
With their ghost inhabitants slipping in through open
Windows, and the light above was a balloon

Drifting to sleep. It was that time, when time was broken
And piecemeal, that identity gained weight,
Fleshed out. It is that time that is woken

In us when we seem to fall or gravitate
Towards each other without knowing it,
A time that is both too early yet late

Enough to be ourselves, the classroom lit
With eyes, the dream working its way through
Troubled nerves, the nightbirds beginning to flit

From haze of branch to haze of branch and the blue-
Indigo of our lives solidifying into selves
We might meet anywhere and address as *you*.

....A Time

Once upon a time when myths were still falling
About us like tall shadows, when you emerged
From infancy and heard the body calling

Out of the fog of the street, and were urged
To follow, at first into the garden, and then
Beyond the gate where the hormones surged

Like crowds of unruly children, half-grown men,
And gusts of sheer energy shook you into fear
And loneliness as is the way with children,

Tumbling forward, so deep within your ear
You could feel the blood gathering then gone
South, into the world, in the spurt of desire.

Mechanics of growth: the yearning to be done
And out before desire is itself, no more
Than pain, embarrassment, anticipation

Of more pain, at the point where the door
Snaps open, beyond the garden, out
In the street and beyond, beyond metaphor

Into body, into flight, into squalor and doubt
And romance. The children run forwards
Like troops into fire hearing a distant shout,

The gunfire of laughter and death. Whose words
Are they speaking? Can you hear your own cry
In the strange cacophony or sound the chords

Of the music where they are shouting? You lie
On your bed. The child is trickling painfully away,
Passing into a future you yourself supply.

I watch from a distance as skinny girls play
Among themselves, I am too young for this.
They move past me laughing. I must stay

In my childhood a while. Already I miss
You. The billowing forth that I anticipate
Is not for me, not yet. I am waiting for your kiss.

The Birds

Sometimes you see a shape that hovers in the eye
And lodges itself in the furniture of the mind,
Part light, part sound, between silence, music and cry

That sings out of half-open drawers. You find
Yourself staring at it through the bedroom door,
Caught in the mirror, perfectly defined

Like your own incomprehensible face but more
Light, more sound. Sometimes I wake and stare
At you beside me as if on a foreign shore,

An object cast there, a figure of the air
Locked into itself, strange, magical
And potent, a burden I can just about bear

To support without the heart breaking, as small
As this one moment in a universe without scale,
And, inside that bright moment, the sum of all

Such moments, years, decades. Outside, frail
Birds are beginning their morning ablution,
Chirruping and squabbling, a musical Braille

That ears may trace and decipher in the commotion
As multiple layers of meaning, your face
More comprehensible than my own, the impression

Of meaning everywhere as superfluous grace,
The windowsill, the sheets, the books by the bed,
The reflection lightly imprinted on the space

Behind a chair, the crumpled clothes, the bedspread
With its foothills, its geologies. The universe
Arrives at the station. The shape of your head

Hangs in the vast forecourt where crowds disperse
And gather like dense flowers, where everything moves
Forward beyond the street, where there is no reverse,

Only, rarely, this blessed stasis: the light that loves
You and holds you still. And slow as dreams,
Birds rise from the roof, swifts, sparrows, thrushes, doves,

As they have always done, their shapes the phonemes
Of a pure language. And you are there, beautiful
As their whistles and slurs, their trilling, their screams.

White Noise

What is the noise of language when words fail?
All language is white noise. It has no grip
On being. It is pure desire, the lost trail

In the wood, the bird's cry, the wrecked ship.
It is as frail as we are, I watch the rain
And hear it skittering. I follow the drip

As it slides down the window again and again,
And the wind goes *I, I, I,* in the door,
Sometimes I imagine the blank terrain

Of the self, its plain windows and bare floor
Beyond which there is an infinity
Of being, and I don't know which scares me more.

At other times the mind is like a city
Of stars and the world is a delirious fever
Like a dream of fecundity

So your eyes want to hoover it up for ever,
And love, since it is love I want to write,
Drifts in the rising dust, lover with lover,

Each a coincidence or trick of the light.
It is language, like desire, that sweeps them on
In the white noise of being. They are in flight.

An time goes roaring by them till they're done
With flying and being. But the words remain
In the air as if they belonged to more or less everyone,

As if they were as common as wind or rain
With everyone outside watching clouds
Form faces, creatures, reading each distant stain.

Bathing and Singing

She sings as she is being bathed.
Widow at eighty-eight. The house sighs
and hovers tactfully in the background
averting its eyes
listening only to this one human sound.

The sun is loafing around the garden.
It is the sun of all her eighty-eight years.
It has no particular axe to grind.
The grass is all ears
and no mouth. The trees don't mind

the music. They gently toss their heads
to keep the time. The voice is coming clean
out of the air at them. Her interpreters eddy
about her. Her unseen
commentators stand by, notebooks at the ready

Primavera

When the chill had lifted, but the afternoon
was not quite warm and it was March, and the sky
was lightening, and it was still too soon
to go without a coat, and there was a dry
edge to the early morning, I rose from myself,
she said, suddenly younger than the calendar,
and tried a few dancing steps as if half-
intoxicated, nor could I help but wonder
whether this dancing was just a peculiar mood
brought on by the faint warmth, or an act
of defiance against time, an attitude
rather than true lightness, dream more than fact,
but it was spring and it seemed right to dance.
What else was there to lose? Why not take the chance,

because winter drags down the day, and we lose
light and waking hours, and time, *she said*, seems
like a hammer in the flesh, and who would choose
such bitterness, if they could help it? Who dreams
of winter as comfort and sweetness? We shrink
away, *she said*, from our very selves, we hold
our lives at a distance and feel we stand at the brink
of a precipice in low light, in the freezing cold,
despite the festivals, the decorations, the songs
and the shows, in an endless February
of mind and body and so it is a person longs
to dance a few steps, for the dance to carry
us through an open door into the back of time
so though we are skidding downhill we seem to climb.

Canzone: In Memoriam WSU

It's no good, sometimes you have to think of it,
the possibility that haunts the idyllic morning
like a morning on the other side of it
but somehow darker, more cussed, as if it
hadn't quite got up but was still asleep,
as if for ever, its eyes tight shut. You know it
in your pyjamas at the mirror. Or you see it
through an open window as it rises and falls
and darkens. And now the wind picks up: rain falls.
You look through the window and feel: *So that's it,
that is what being over is like, just like a cloud,
a cloud riding in on top of another cloud.*

Or else you ignore it, accept a different cloud,
the one of unknowing, and simply trust it,
crying out to the face that rides the cloud,
following its drift, taking notice of cloud-
shapes, reading clouds, reading the morning
for rain, the grace of rain, the heart of cloud.
It is as if you were walking through a cloud
of words while word itself was asleep
and dreaming you. As if the word could sleep!
As if words fell out of a mysterious cloud!
And look outside now, watch as rain falls
like grace on everything that rises and falls.

Out in the war-torn world a body falls.
The streets are all smoke and cloud.
You're on your motorbike as night falls
across the valley, or is it a bomb that falls?
You dream and there is the strangeness of it,
the dream, the memory that, like a pattern, falls
into place and becomes familiar. Man falls
into dream, world into room: the ritual of morning
with its alarm clock; the regular morning.
And here too the rain is falling fast. It falls
far and near, on life, on death. It falls while we sleep,
as if rain itself were merely a falling asleep.

How easy it is sometimes to fall asleep.
Power falls, time falls, body falls, then life too falls:
it falls with pain, indignity, with broken sleep,
brief wakefulness that's followed by light sleep
and lighter memory. Youth is an electric cloud
full of lightning. Sometimes it strikes in sleep,
the fullness of it pressing against sleep
then bursting into light and sound. How it
dazzles as if all life were dazzling. Can it
ever have been so bright, disturbing our sleep?
Once life was forever moving into morning,
yesterday morning to tomorrow morning.

And so there is always something that is morning,
something of morning about us. Fast asleep,
we wake of a sudden. The body cries morning:
the clock, the birds, the light, whatever is morning
arrives in a rush, in a thunder of footfalls
on the bare boards of consciousness where morning
is setting out furniture. Welcome, brisk morning!
Body withers and fades, disperses like cloud
but memory has its own way with cloud,
seeking the light inside it, looking for morning.
Look it is there, it exclaims. Look! Can you see it?
And morning is there, and all the mornings beyond it.

Now, look, can you see him? What is it
moving there like a man in a body of cloud?
Clouds weep, we say, being human. *When rain falls,
clouds are weeping*. So language shifts in sleep,
and then we wake and soon enough it is morning.

Pools

1

Out of the birthing-pool
        into this cool
                slab of medicated glass
                        the bodies pass.

In city basements, in tall
        complexes, breast-stroke and crawl
                and dive bomb and high
                        board and shrill cry,
                                they press by.

We are water-borne,
        clothes-shorn,
                in fish-school,
                        in birthing-pool.

2

In fish-school,   in birthing-pool
in hot, sulphurous,   steaming
undergrounds of   the imagination,
agencies   are scheming.

Under domes,   between pillars,
on marble steps   the nations
dissolve   into private
whispered   assignations.

Budapest waters   run deep,
seethe   upward from rock,
then settle   in their basins
like a furious stopped   clock.

3

Here the genders divide
  day by alternate day.
    Mothers and daughters arrive
      enter the pool and stay

an hour or two gently pushing
forward into warm
intensity that replicates
form for form.

The men next day hang
in the dark, part submerged
trees, their voices low
and clear as if purged

of some higher frequency,
fathers and sons, their hot
energies not so much sunk
as rooted to the spot.

4

Water-borne, clothes-shorn,
the bathers have gone.

Water sulks and settles,
folding petals.

But in navel and fontanelle
something continues, the swell

of a tide stopped,
the temperature dropped.

You feel it in your chest too, the thrust
withheld, an accumulated dust

of fine spray, a deserted quarter
of lost deep water,

so you move on, the back of your throat
faintly dry, keeping neatly afloat,

pressing forward, air-gowned,
air-fed and undrowned.

The Man Who Wove Grass

1

The man who wove grass made himself a wardrobe
fit for the summer when grass was all he'd need
to dress in, when no icy wind would probe

his warps and wefts, so that his head might bleed
the memories that left him dumb, undreamt,
as if that grass, the marram and the weed

might bind a wound and stop a mouth, or tempt
nature back into the place he'd known once,
in mist-blanketed fields, in ponds, in unkempt

gardens, among horses, in the governance
of creatures fed and watered, in pale
blear dawns, as if grass, by some chance

could be what his mouth was, his mouth stale
with refuse as he went about on hands and knees,
his mouth to the ground, leaving a faint trail

of grief behind him. He lay under trees
knitting grass vests, weaving socks of grass,
grass boots, grass berets, grass jerkins and puttees,

swathing himself in the uniform of loss
in a premature interment, it was said,
and there'd be some grass mausoleum or palace

with a plaque for him as for the other dead
under the grass, because nature without human
agency was just nature, and nature's teeth were red.

2

I knew a boy who used to stare at grass
imagining a consolation. The quick
life of the ant moving to a compass

of natural necessity: that was the trick
he had to master and it was as if his mind
were entirely of grass with its own traffic

101

of determined creatures, not merely a blind
rush towards collapse but a serene
intuited death to which anyone might resign

himself, part of a universal green
that covered the earth: earthworm, ladybird,
money spider, the brilliant sheen

of the bluebottle as it drifted and blurred
towards a single blade to land
a moment, then push off, with that thick furred

sound, drubbing the air like a small hand
worn into transparency, or a fish-scale
fallen from the sky and trying to rise while fanned

and thrust by the wind. He saw the pale
world of soil as a map out of which grew
great lush jungles working down a trail

more amenable to his anxieties, a world true
to itself and just in its peculiar fashion
to what its inhabitants were obliged to do.

3

Grass that leaves a smear on trousers, on knees
and elbows, already cladding us for war
and interment; grass cheap under trees,

grown damp in late hours; the grass floor
of childhood forests where armies
of shadows move in formations, yet more

grass between paving stones, down alleys,
poking through walls, through slithering mud
obliterating entire families;

grass that grows inward, thickening the blood
and lining the bones; grass that cushions the skull
from within; grass that seems to flood

from orifices, meadows of grass that billow and muscle
through the gut; grass trembling with fear
in the deluge, lightning illuminated under a full

sky in the head; grass that gathers in the ear
to prevent it splitting; grass luxuriant
in the lungs and forever settling there;

grass that is madness, that spreads slant
in the heart's wind, against the throbbing door
of the heart, pressing and exuberant;

grass on which we lie flat out to restore
some sense of balance against the sky
with its alien birds and uneasy pallor.

4

The man who wove grass moved through a world of blades
without effort, as if grass were no more than green water
and he an expert swimmer through various shades

of green. Such innocent madness did not matter
to the world since he was one of many veterans
of indeterminate age, escaping the clatter

of general warfare. He wove according patterns
and patterns were soothing. He was his own mother,
doing up his own floral buttons.

Grass parted for him then drew together
behind him as water does. It was his element.
He knew its delicate touch, the light-as-feather

sweep as it moved aside, its resilient
and flexible habit of rising again after drought,
after flood, after fire, after almost any event

you could imagine. Grass allowed no doubt.
It was closing over him even now, as certain
as the air he was breathing calmly in and out.

Woolworths

It was dark, a Wednesday morning, and the store
was half sealed-off in the infinite melancholy
of small pickings. Wrapping paper, a score
of remnant CDs, barely enough to load a trolley.
Garden fitments, stationery... all the grand spaces
of the humble, vacated. There stood the childhoods:
the sweet counter, the scribbling pad, the lost faces
of the faintly bored dispensing their gentle goods.

Worlds swell, explode, shed light, draw darkness in.
A match blows out in the draught. Nothing will keep.
A plastic pencil case abandoned in the bin
lifts a helpless lid but makes no unnecessary fuss.
Fire, firelighters, matchboxes, ashtrays... Cheap
vanishings. Cheap days. We'll be the death of us.